P9-DFQ-942

Casseroles
to the Rescue

*Easy-To-Make
Home-Cooked
Casseroles*

Barbara C. Jones

Casseroles To The Rescue

1st Printing May 2003
2nd Printing July 2003

Copyright © 2001
By Cookbook Resources LLC, Highland Village, Texas.
All rights reserved

ISBN 1-931294-42-9
Paperback ISBN 1-931294-50-X

Library of Congress Number: 2003103580

All Rights Reserved. No part of this book may be reproduced in any form
without written permission from the publisher, except for brief passages
included in a review appearing in a newspaper or magazine with
permission from the publisher.

Illustrated by Nancy Murphy Griffith
Art Direction by Liz Reinken

Edited, Designed, Published and Manufactured in the
United States of America by
Cookbook Resources, LLC
541 Doubletree Drive
Highland Village, Texas 75077
Toll free 866-229-2665
www.cookbookresources.com

Flavors
of Home™
Preserving
The Family Meal

cookbook
resources® LLC

Introduction

Recipes in this cookbook are mostly family recipes that are easy enough for everyday, but nice enough for company and friends for weekend entertaining. These dishes are great for potlucks, new neighbors, church suppers, supper clubs and fun socials.

They are easy recipes because they don't require lots of preparation time or special ingredients. You probably have all the ingredients in your kitchen already, but if you have to go to the grocery store, the ingredients will be easy to find.

They are also versatile, colorful and sometimes modern adaptations of old family recipes many of us enjoyed in our early years. And they are tasty and delicious enough to be modern family classics, those meals that kids and parents request over and over and through time become favorite food memories.

And Salads Too…As an added addition to our outstanding casserole recipes, we have added several great salad recipes that are new, different and a little out of the ordinary. They are tasty accompaniments to our casseroles and make any meal complete.

We hope you enjoy this wonderful collection of everyday and entertaining recipes that will make your life easier and your dinners as happy as can be.

Enjoy!

Barbara C. Jones

Contents

These dishes are wonderful for late morning breakfasts or late-night snacks. The best thing about them is you can make them ahead of time and pull them out of the freezer when you're ready.

Here are some different pasta dishes, super veggies and rice dishes that go with any entrée you have. They all make perfect accompaniments.

Delicious casseroles for all vegetables make this section a blessing. Dress up any vegetable and make it the "centerpiece" of your meal.

There are no ordinary chicken dishes in this section. Each has a its own distinct flavor, colorful combination of vegetables and pastas and special delicious tastes.

From heavy to light, spicy to regular, these beef casseroles join the ranks of everyday favorites and anticipated main dishes.

Casserole Dish Sizes

Choosing casserole dishes today is lots of fun, but may be a little confusing because there are so many different shapes and sizes. Listed below are the most common, but don't hesitate to try a beautiful dish with a lid and handles that would look great on your table.

One of the best things about casseroles is that you serve the dish in the same dish in which you cooked it. If the dish has handles, it makes serving much easier and the clean-up is limited. If you only get one casserole or baking dish, your best bet is probably the 13 x 9 x 2-inch baking dish. Most of the casseroles in this book work with this dish. We've also listed several casseroles that are big enough, you may make 2 smaller casseroles and freeze one for a later date.

Dish Sizes	Approximate Volume
8 x 8 x 2 square	8 cups
11 x 7 x 2 rectangular	8 cups
9 x 9 x 2 rectangular	10 cups
13 x 9 x 2 rectangular	15 cups
1-quart casserole	4 cups
2-quart casserole	8 cups
2 1/2-quart casserole	10 cups
3-quart casserole	12 cups

Casserole Freezing Tips

The best way to save time and money is to make a large casserole, put it into 2 smaller dishes and freeze one for another day. When you have an extra casserole in the freezer, you'll never be caught without a meal ready to go. Freezing suggestions are listed with most of the recipes in this cookbook. Here are a few more helpful tips for freezing casseroles.

1. Always let casserole cool before freezing.
2. Reduce cooking time of casserole by 10 to 20 minutes, so it will not dry out when it is reheated.
3. Always cover the casserole before putting it in the freezer.
4. If the final ingredients are added to the top of the casserole for added "crunch" (potato chips, fried onion rings), don't freeze it, but wait to add it when you reheat it.
5. Use an oven-to-freezer container so you don't have to change dishes.
6. Reduce the seasonings slightly because they may intensify with time.
7. Store in freezer no more than 2 to 4 weeks to maintain freshness and moisture.
8. Defrost in refrigerator.

Brunch Casseroles

An Apple for Breakfast

4-5 tart cooking apples, peeled, sliced
¾ cup chopped pecans
½ cup golden raisins
6 tablespoons packed brown sugar
½ teaspoon ground cinnamon
¼ cup (½ stick) margarine
6 eggs
1 ½ cups orange juice
1 cup flour
¾ teaspoon salt
3 tablespoons sugar
Extra cinnamon
Maple syrup

- In large skillet, saute apples, pecans, raisins, brown sugar, cinnamon and margarine until apples begin to soften, about 6 minutes and stir often.
- Place in a buttered 9 x 13-inch baking dish.
- In mixing bowl, combine eggs, orange juice, flour and salt, beat slowly until mixture is smooth and stir around edges of bowl.
- Pour over apple mixture. Sprinkle with 3 tablespoons sugar and a little cinnamon.
- Bake uncovered at 400° for about 20 to 25 minutes or until a knife inserted near the center of casserole comes out clean. Serve with maple syrup.

This is a really neat breakfast casserole to go along with your "bacon and eggs" and a delicious way to serve fruit with breakfast or brunch!

Breakfast Tortillas

¾ cup chopped onion
¼ cup (½ stick) margarine
¼ cup flour
¾ cup milk
1 pint half-and-half cream
1 (7 ounce) can chopped green chilies
1 teaspoon salt
½ teaspoon white pepper
10 eggs
3 avocados
Salt to taste
8 (8 inch) flour tortillas
1 (8 ounce) package shredded monterey jack cheese
Salsa

- In a large skillet, saute onion in the margarine. Stir in flour; cook on low 1 minute while stirring constantly. Add milk and cream; cook on medium heat, stirring constantly until mixture has thickened.
- Add green chilies, salt, pepper and garlic powder. Remove sauce from heat and set aside.
- In another skillet, scramble eggs lightly; remove from heat.
- In small bowl, mash the avocados; sprinkle with a little salt.
- Spread out all tortillas on counter and spoon 2 tablespoons of the sauce, ⅛ of the eggs and ⅛ of the avocados on each tortilla.
- Roll up and place seam side down on a greased 9 x 13-inch baking dish. Spoon remaining sauce over tortillas.
- Bake covered at 325° for about 25 minutes or just until tortillas are hot and bubbly.
- Remove from oven, sprinkle cheese over top and return to oven for about 10 minutes. When serving, top each tortilla with a dab of salsa.

To remove tortillas from baking pan, always use a long,
wide spatula so that the tortillas do not break up.

Breakfast Bake

1 pound hot sausage, cooked, crumbled
2 tablespoons dried onion flakes
1 cup shredded cheddar cheese
1 cup biscuit mix
¼ teaspoon salt
¼ teaspoon black pepper
5 eggs
2 cups milk

- Place cooked and crumbled sausage in a Pam sprayed 9 x 13-inch baking dish. Sprinkle with onion flakes and cheese.
- In mixing bowl, combine biscuit mix, salt, pepper and eggs. Beat well with fork (not mixer). Add milk, stir until fairly smooth and pour over sausage mixture.
- Bake covered for 35 minutes.

If you want to make one day and cook the next morning, add an extra 5 minutes cooking time since you would be taking it right out of the refrigerator.

To use this recipe for a brunch or morning bridge club, just add 1 (8 ounce) can whole kernel corn, drained, to make it a little heartier.

Overnight Breakfast

7 cups small cubed French bread, bottom crust removed
¾ cup chopped pecans
1 (3 ounce) package cream cheese, softened
4 tablespoons sugar
1 (8 ounce) carton whipping cream
½ cup real maple syrup
6 eggs, slightly beaten
1 teaspoon vanilla
½ teaspoon ground cinnamon
¼ teaspoon salt
Additional maple syrup

- Place cubed bread in greased 9 x 13-inch baking dish and press down gently. Sprinkle with pecans.
- In mixing bowl, beat cream cheese and sugar until fluffy and gradually mix in whipping cream and syrup.
- In a separate bowl whisk together eggs, vanilla, cinnamon and salt and fold into cream cheese-whipping cream mixture. Slowly pour this mixture evenly over bread.
- Cover and refrigerate overnight.
- Remove from refrigerator 20 minutes before baking.
- Bake covered at 350° for 30 minutes or until center is set and top is golden brown. To serve, cut into squares and serve with maple syrup.

This is "French toast" the easy way and it's not just for company!
The kids will love it too.

Quick Breakfast Sandwiches

8 slices white bread*
Softened margarine
2 cups cooked, finely chopped ham
1 cup shredded Swiss cheese
3 eggs, beaten
1 ⅔ cups milk
1 tablespoon dried, minced onion flakes
1 teaspoon prepared mustard
½ teaspoon salt

- Trim crusts off bread slices. Spread margarine on 1 side of each slice of bread. Place 4 slices in a buttered 8-inch square baking pan.
- Top bread slices with chopped ham and top with remaining bread slices, buttered side up. Sprinkle with shredded Swiss cheese.
- In bowl combine eggs, milk, onion flakes, prepared mustard and salt and mix well. Slowly pour over bread slices. Cover and refrigerate overnight or at least 8 hours.
- Remove baking pan from refrigerator about 10 minutes before cooking. Bake uncovered at 325° for 30 minutes or until center is set. To serve, cut into 4 sandwiches.

*Wouldn't the kids love to say they had sandwiches for breakfast! ?
What a cool Mom!*

* Use regular bread slices, not thin sandwich slices.

Elegant Eggs

¼ cup (½ stick) butter
6 tablespoons flour
2 teaspoons dried dill weed
½ cup dry white wine
½ cup clam juice
1 ½ cups whipping cream
1 ¼ cups grated parmesan cheese
14 hard-boiled eggs
2 (6 ounce) cans shrimp, drained, deveined
1 ½ cups dry breadcrumbs
1 teaspoon Creole seasoning
⅛ cup (¼ stick) butter, melted
Sprigs of fresh dill

- In saucepan, melt butter and stir in flour and dill weed. Cook on medium heat for about 2 minutes, but do not brown.
- Stir in wine, clam juice and cream and cook, stirring constantly, until sauce thickens. Stir in parmesan cheese and set aside.
- Cut eggs in half lengthwise and place eggs, yolk side up, in buttered, shallow baking dish.
- Cover with shrimp and pour sauce over top of shrimp.
- Combine breadcrumbs, Creole seasoning and melted butter. Sprinkle on top of sauce-covered shrimp. Let stand at room temperature for 30 minutes.
- Bake uncovered at 375° for 20 minutes or until casserole is hot and bubbly. Garnish with sprigs of fresh dill.

Fiesta Eggs

1 pound sausage
½ green bell pepper, chopped
½ sweet red bell pepper, chopped
3 green onions, chopped
1 (10 ounce) can tomatoes and green chilies
½ cup hot, chunky salsa
4 ounces cubed processed cheese
10 eggs, slightly beaten
1½ teaspoons salt
½ cup sour cream
⅔ cup milk

- In skillet, slowly brown sausage, bell peppers and onions. Spoon sausage-onion mixture onto paper towels, drain and set aside.
- Dry skillet with more paper towels, pour tomatoes, green chilies, salsa and processed cheese in skillet and cook, stirring constantly, only until cheese melts. Remove from heat.
- In bowl beat together eggs, salt, sour cream and milk and fold in sausage mixture and tomato-cheese mixture. Transfer to greased 7 x 11-inch baking dish.
- Bake uncovered at 325° for about 25 minutes or until center is set.

Bacon & Eggs Anyone?

2 potatoes, peeled, cubed
¼ cup (½ stick) margarine
¼ cup flour
1 pint half-and-half cream
1 (16 ounce) package shredded cheddar cheese
1 teaspoon dried Italian seasoning
½ teaspoon salt
½ teaspoon white pepper
12 hard-boiled eggs, sliced
1 pound bacon, cooked, slightly crumbled
1 ½ cups breadcrumbs
3 tablespoons margarine, melted

- Cook potatoes in salted water just until tender, but do not overcook. Drain well.
- In large saucepan melt ¼ cup (½ stick) margarine and stir in flour. Cook, stirring constantly, 1 minute or until smooth.
- Gradually add cream and cook over medium heat, stirring constantly, until sauce thickens.
- Add cheddar cheese, Italian seasoning, salt and white pepper, stirring constantly, until cheese melts. Remove from heat.
- In buttered 9 x 13-inch baking dish, layer half of egg slices, half of bacon and half of cheese sauce.
- Spoon potatoes over cheese sauce and top with remaining egg slices, bacon and cheese sauce. Combine breadcrumbs and 3 tablespoons melted margarine. Sprinkle over top of casserole.
- Cover and refrigerate overnight.

- Before baking remove casserole from refrigerator and let stand for about 20 minutes. Uncover and bake at 350º for 30 minutes.

This casserole is also great for a late night supper. You really don't need anything else with it except biscuits or toast.

Baked Stuffed Eggs

6 hard-boiled eggs
½ cup fresh very finely chopped mushrooms caps
3 tablespoons butter
1 tablespoon white wine worcestershire sauce
¼ teaspoon salt
2-3 dashes Tabasco

Cheese Sauce
3 tablespoons butter
3 tablespoons flour
¾ cup milk
⅔ cup shredded cheddar cheese
½ cup seasoned breadcrumbs

- Split eggs lengthwise. Remove yolks and mash.
- Saute mushrooms in butter. Add mushrooms and seasonings to yolks and mix well.
- Stuff into egg-white shells and arrange in buttered, shallow casserole dish.

To make Cheese Sauce:
- In saucepan, combine butter and flour and cook on medium heat just until butter and flour are well mixed.
- Add milk slowly and cook, stirring constantly, until mixture is smooth and thick. Remove from heat, fold in cheese and stir until cheese melts.
- Pour cheese sauce over eggs and sprinkle with breadcrumbs.
- Bake uncovered at 350° for 20 minutes.

Tortilla Egg Rolls

½ sliced fresh mushrooms
1 onion, chopped
½ cup chopped green bell pepper
½ cup chopped sweet red bell pepper
¼ cup (½ stick) margarine
6 eggs
1 ½ cups half-and-half cream, divided
½ teaspoon salt
¼ teaspoon white pepper
1 cup fully cooked, shredded ham
1(10 ounce) can cream of mushroom soup, divided
8-10 (8-inch) flour tortillas
1 ½ cups shredded cheddar cheese

- In large skillet, saute mushrooms, onion and both bell peppers in the margarine and set aside.
- In separate bowl, whisk together eggs, ½ cup cream, salt and white pepper and add shredded ham. Pour egg-ham mixture into skillet with mushroom-pepper mixture.
- Cook, stirring constantly, over medium heat until eggs are almost set and not dry. (Do not overcook eggs.)
- In buttered 9 x 13-inch baking dish, spread half of the soup over bottom of baking dish.
- Spread tortillas out on counter and place 3 tablespoons egg-ham mixture down center of each tortilla, then sprinkle each with 1 tablespoon cheese. Roll up and place-seam side down over the soup.
- Mix remaining soup with 1 cup cream and pour over tortillas.
- Bake covered at 325° for about 25 minutes or until tortillas are heated thoroughly.
- Remove from oven and sprinkle remaining cheese over top of casserole. Return to oven for 5 minutes or until cheese melts.

You can remove these rolls "in tact" from the baking pan with a long, wide spatula. If you use a spoon to remove rolls, they will tear up easily.

Sausage Quiche

1 (9-inch) deep dish uncooked pie shell
1 (7 ounce) can whole green chilies
1 pound hot sausage, cooked, crumbled
4 eggs, slightly beaten
2 cups half-and-half cream
½ cup grated parmesan cheese
¾ cup grated Swiss cheese
½ teaspoon salt
¼ teaspoon pepper

- Line bottom of pie shell with split and seeded green chilies. Sprinkle sausage over chilies.
- Combine eggs, cream, both cheeses, salt and pepper. Slowly pour over sausage.
- Cover edge of pastry with a thin strip of foil to prevent excessive browning.
- Bake at 350° for 35 minutes or until center is set and golden brown. Allow quiche to set at room temperature for 5 minutes before slicing to serve.

Quick Quiche

½ cup (1 stick) margarine, melted
1 ½ cups half-and-half cream
½ teaspoon salt
¼ teaspoon pepper
3 green onions, with tops, chopped
½ cup biscuit mix
1 cup grated Swiss cheese
¾ cup chopped ham
4 eggs, beaten

- Grease a 10-inch deep pie plate.
- Combine melted margarine, cream, salt, pepper, green onions and biscuit mix. Blend well with mixer and pour into pie plate.
- Sprinkle batter with cheese and ham. Push meat below the surface with back of spoon
- Beat eggs in same mixing bowl and pour over ham and cheese.
- Bake at 350° for 35 minutes or until center is set.
- Allow to set at room temperature about 10 minutes before slicing.

Quesadilla Pie

1 (4 ounce) can chopped green chilies
½ pound sausage, cooked, crumbled
2 cups shredded cheddar cheese
3 eggs, well beaten
1 ½ cups milk
¾ cup biscuit mix
Hot salsa

- Sprinkle green chilies in sprayed 9-inch pie pan. Add layer of cooked sausage and layer of cheddar cheese.
- In separate bowl, combine eggs, milk and biscuit mix and mix well.
- Slowly pour over chilies, sausage and cheese.
- Bake at 350° for 35 minutes or until center is set. Serve with salsa on top of each slice.

*To give this "pie" a little more zip, use hot sausage
and a few drops of Tabasco!*

Chiffon-Cheese Souffle

12 slices white bread, crust removed*
2 (5 ounce) jars Old English cheese spread, softened
6 eggs, beaten
3 cups milk
¾ cup (1 ½ sticks) margarine, melted
½ teaspoon salt

- Be sure to use a dish with high sides because souffle will rise and fall slightly. The baking dish will be full.
- Cut each slice of bread into 4 triangles and spoon dab of cheese on each.
- Place triangles evenly in layers in sprayed 9 x 13-inch baking dish.
- Combine eggs, milk, margarine and salt and mix well. Slowly pour mixture over layers of bread.
- Cover and chill 8 hours.
- Remove from refrigerator about 20 minutes before baking.
- Bake uncovered at 350° for 1 hour.

Wow! Is this ever good. It is light and fluffy, but still very rich. It must be the Old English cheese that gives it that special cheese flavor. This recipe is placed in the Brunch section, but it can easily be served at lunch. It is even good left-over and warmed up.

Be sure to use regular slices, not thin slices.

Hot Tamale-Cheese Fiesta

2 (13 ounce) jars beef tamales with sauce
1 (10 ounce) can cream of mushroom soup
2 teaspoons taco seasoning
1 (8 ounce) package shredded Mexican-cheese blend,
divided

- Drain sauce from jar of tamales into cup and set aside. Pour tamales onto a plate and remove paper from tamales.
- Place tamales, side by side, in a baking dish. Sprinkle ¼ of cheese over top of tamales.
- Combine ½ cup sauce from tamales, mushroom soup and taco seasoning and mix well.
- Pour sauce mixture over tamales and cheese.
- Bake at 350° for 5 to 10 minutes to heat tamales thoroughly.
- Remove from oven and pour ½ of remaining cheese over top and heat until cheese melts.

Sausage-Apple Ring

2 pounds bulk sausage
1 ½ cups crushed cracker crumbs
2 eggs, slightly beaten
½ cup milk
¼ cup minced onion
1 cup very finely chopped apple
Scrambled eggs

- Thoroughly combine sausage, cracker crumbs, eggs, milk, onion and chopped apple. (This will require a good bit of mixing to get everything worked into the sausage.)
- Press into 9-inch ring mold. (Press well because you will have holes in the bottom if sausage is not pressed down well.)
- With knife, ease around top of edge and center edge of ring mold and turn onto shallow baking pan or sheet cake pan with edges.
- Bake at 350° for 45 minutes, then drain off fat. (The best way I have found to drain the fat off and to get the ring on a serving plate is to spoon off the fat in center of ring, then take several paper towels and place around the ring, letting the towels take up the fat around the edges. Let cool a little.)
- Lay a plate, up side down on top of ring. Flip again and your ring center will be ready to be filled with the eggs.
- Cover and refrigerate.
- For breakfast the next morning, just reheat ring for about 15 minutes.
- While ring is reheating, scramble about a dozen eggs and fill center of ring.

This is a fun way to serve scrambled eggs and sausage! Your guests will really be impressed! It sounds like a lot of trouble, but it really isn't. You are just doing a lot of flipping.

Green Chili Puff

10 eggs
½ cup flour
1 teaspoon baking powder
½ teaspoon salt
1 (16 ounce) carton small curd cottage cheese
1 (8 ounce) package shredded monterey jack cheese
1 bunch green onions and tops, chopped
1 (8 ounce) package shredded cheddar cheese
½ cup (1 stick) margarine, melted
1 (7 ounce) can chopped green chilies

- In bowl, beat eggs until light and lemon colored. Add flour, baking powder and salt and beat until smooth.
- Add cottage cheese, mozzarella cheese, green onions, cheddar cheese, margarine and green chilies. Stir until well mixed.
- Pour into buttered 9 x 13-inch baking dish.
- Bake uncovered at 350° for 40 minutes or until top is slightly brown around edges and center appears firm. Serve immediately. Salsa may be served on the side.

This recipe is so versatile! You can cut it in little squares and serve warm as an appetizer. For brunch or for lunch. It goes well with any Mexican meal, morning, noon or night.

Ranch Sausage and Grits

1 cup instant grits
1 pound hot sausage
½ teaspoon minced garlic
1 (8 ounce) package shredded sharp cheddar cheese, divided
½ cup hot salsa
¼ cup (½ stick) margarine, melted
2 eggs, beaten

- Cook instant grits in 2 cups boiling water according to package directions.
- In skillet, brown and cook sausage and garlic and drain.
- Combine cooked grits, sausage, half the cheese, salsa, melted margarine and eggs and mix well.
- Pour into buttered 9 x 13-inch baking dish.
- Bake uncovered at 350° for 50 minutes. Remove from oven and sprinkle remaining cheese over casserole. Return to oven for 10 minutes.

Can you find a tall, lanky Texan to invite to breakfast? He'll be putty in your hands if you serve him this sausage and grits.

Curried Fruit Medley

1 (29 ounce) can sliced peaches, drained
2 (15 ounce) cans pineapple chunks, drained
1 (10 ounce) jar maraschino cherries, drained
1 cup packed brown sugar
1 teaspoon curry powder
¼ cup (½ stick) margarine, cut into pieces

- Pour fruit in 9 x 13-inch baking dish.
- Combine brown sugar and curry and stir well. Sprinkle over fruit and dot with margarine.
- Bake covered at 350° for 30 minutes or until thoroughly heated and bubbly around edges.

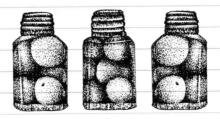

Pineapple-Cheese Casserole

1 (20 ounce) can pineapple chunks, drained
1 cup sugar
5 tablespoons flour
1 ½ cups shredded cheddar cheese
1 stack round, buttery crackers, crushed
½ cup (1 stick) margarine, melted

- Butter 9 x 13-inch baking dish and layer in following order: pineapple, sugar-flour mixture, shredded cheese and cracker crumbs.
- Drizzle melted margarine over casserole.
- Bake uncovered at 350º for 25 minutes or until bubbly.

This is really a wonderful and different combination of flavors. It is great served at brunch or great served with a sandwich at lunch.

Breakfast-Ready Casserole

6 English muffins, halved
1 pound hot sausage, cooked, drained
1 (8 ounce) package shredded cheddar-jack cheese, divided
5 eggs, beaten
1 (10 ounce) can cream of mushroom soup
2 ½ cups milk

- Line sprayed 9 x 13-inch baking dish with English muffins halves and sprinkle cooked sausage.
- In separate bowl combine half the cheese, eggs, soup and milk and mix well.
- Gently pour cheese-soup mixture over sausage and muffins. Sprinkle remaining cheese over top of casserole.
- Bake at 325° for 65 to 70 minutes. Test to be sure center of casserole is set.
- Let set for 10 or 15 minutes before slicing and serving.

Side Dishes

Spinach-Cheese Manicotti

Side Dishes

1 onion, minced
2 teaspoons minced garlic
2 tablespoons oil
1 (15 ounce) carton ricotta cheese
1 (3 ounce) package cream cheese, softened
1 (8 ounce) package shredded mozzarella cheese, divided
1 (3 ounce) package grated parmesan cheese, divided
2 teaspoons Italian seasoning
½ teaspoon salt
½ teaspoon black pepper
1 (10 ounce) box frozen chopped spinach, thawed, drained
9 manicotti shells, cooked, drained on wax paper
1 (26 ounce) jar spaghetti sauce

- In skillet, saute onion and garlic in oil and set aside,
- In mixing bowl, combine ricotta, cream cheese, half the mozzarella, half the parmesan cheese, Italian seasoning, salt and pepper and beat until well mixed.
- Drain spinach with several paper towels and squeeze until spinach is well drained.
- Add spinach and onion to cheese mixture and mix well.
- Spoon this mixture into manicotti shells (using 1 teaspoon at a time). Be careful not to tear shells.
- Pour half of spaghetti sauce in bottom of greased 9 x 13-inch baking dish. Arrange shells over the sauce and top with remaining sauce.
- Cover and bake at 350° for 30 minutes. Remove from oven, uncover and sprinkle remaining cheeses over top. Return to oven just until cheese melts.

This does take a little extra time to fill the shells, but it is really a special dish and well worth the time it takes!

Confetti Orzo

8 ounces orzo pasta

½ cup (1 stick) butter

3 cups broccoli florets, stemmed

1 bunch green onions and tops, chopped

1 sweet red bell pepper, seeded, chopped

2 cups chopped celery

1 clove garlic, minced

½ teaspoon cumin

2 teaspoons chicken bouillon

1 (8 ounce) carton sour cream

1 (16 ounce) jar creamy alfredo sauce

1 teaspoon seasoned salt

1 teaspoon white pepper

- Cook orzo according to package directions, however, it is best to stir orzo several times during cooking time. Drain.
- While orzo is cooking, melt butter in skillet and saute broccoli, onions, red bell pepper, celery, garlic and cumin and cook just until tender-crisp.
- Add chicken bouillon to vegetables.
- Spoon into large bowl and fold in sour cream, alfredo sauce, seasoned salt, white pepper and orzo. Spoon into buttered 9 x 13-inch baking dish.
- This is ready to be cooked, but you may refrigerate it and cook later. After it has come to room temperature, cook covered at 325° for 30 minutes.

This is really good. The alfredo sauce gives it a very mild, pleasing flavor. (Sure beats "buttered rice".) This can easily be made into a main dish by adding 3 to 4 cups chopped, cooked chicken or turkey.

Carnival Couscous

1 (5.7 ounce) box herbed chicken couscous
¼ cup (½ stick) margarine
1 sweet red bell pepper, cut in tiny pieces
1 yellow squash, seeded, cut in tiny pieces
1 cup fresh broccoli flowerets, finely chopped
1 cup chopped celery
½ teaspoon seasoned salt
½ teaspoon white pepper

- Cook couscous according to package directions, but omit butter called for on box.
- With margarine in saucepan, saute bell pepper, squash, broccoli and celery and cook about 10 minutes or until vegetables are almost tender.
- Combine couscous, vegetables and seasonings and serve.
- (If you want to make this in advance, place couscous and vegetables in buttered baking dish and mix well. Bake covered at 325° for about 20 minutes.)

Take a back seat Rice! Couscous is here! Couscous is an ideal side dish for any entree because it absorbs flavors as it soaks up liquid. Couscous is a fine, tiny, round Middle Eastern pasta that is often thought of as a grain.

Curried Couscous

1 ½ cups chicken broth
½ cup golden raisins
1 teaspoon curry powder
¼ teaspoon salt
1 cup uncooked couscous
⅓ cup oil
2 tablespoons lemon juice
1 teaspoon sugar
½ cup slivered almonds, toasted
2 fresh green onions, sliced

- In saucepan, combine chicken broth, raisins, curry powder and salt and bring to a boil.
- Remove from heat and stir in couscous. Cover and let stand 5 minutes. Fluff with a fork and cook, uncovered.
- Combine oil, lemon juice, sugar and almonds and toss with couscous.
- Sprinkle green onion over top and serve.

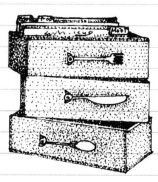

Sensational Spaghetti

½ cup (1 stick) butter
1 ½ teaspoons minced garlic
1 (12 ounce) package thin spaghetti
1 cup grated parmesan cheese
1 pint whipping cream
1 teaspoon dried parsley flakes
½ teaspoon seasoned salt
½ teaspoon white pepper
10-12 strips bacon, fried crisp, crumbled

- In large skillet, melt butter and saute garlic until slightly browned. Cook spaghetti according to package directions and drain.
- Add spaghetti, parmesan cheese, cream, parsley flakes, salt and pepper and mix well.
- Spoon into buttered 2-quart baking dish. Cover and bake at 325° just until it is warm, about 15 minutes.
- Uncover and sprinkle crumbled bacon over casserole.

Forget the tomato sauce. This is spaghetti to love!

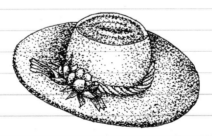

Pasta Frittata

1 onion, chopped
1 green bell pepper, chopped
1 sweet red bell pepper, chopped
2 tablespoons (¼ stick) margarine
1 (7 ounce) box thin spaghetti, slightly broken, cooked
1 (8 ounce) package shredded mozzarella cheese
5 eggs
1 cup milk
⅓ cup shredded parmesan cheese
1 tablespoon dried basil
1 teaspoon oregano
1 teaspoon seasoned salt
½ teaspoon white pepper

- In skillet, saute onion and both peppers in margarine over medium heat for about 5 minutes, but do not brown.
- In large bowl combine onion-pepper mixture and spaghetti and toss. Add mozzarella cheese and toss.
- In separate bowl, beat eggs, milk, parmesan cheese, basil, oregano, seasoned salt and pepper. Add spaghetti mixture and pour into buttered 9 x 13-inch baking dish.
- Cover with foil and bake at 375° for about 15 to 20 minutes. Uncover and make sure eggs are set. If not, bake 2 to 3 minutes longer.

This can be put together, refrigerated and baked later. Let it get to room temperature before placing in oven. Cut into squares to serve. It is a great dish for a luncheon or late night supper.

Mushroom Pasta

1 onion, chopped
1 cup chopped celery
1 sweet red bell pepper, chopped
1 green bell pepper, chopped
6 tablespoons (¾ stick) margarine
1 ⅓ cups orzo pasta
1 (14 ounce) can beef broth
1 cup water
1 (7 ounce) can sliced mushrooms, drained
1 tablespoon worcestershire sauce
½ teaspoon salt
¾ cup chopped walnuts
Chopped green onions for garnish

- Saute onion, celery, bell pepper in margarine.
- Cook orzo in beef broth and water for 10 to 11 minutes and drain.
- In large bowl, combine onion-bell pepper mixture, orzo, mushrooms, worcestershire, salt, pepper and walnuts and mix well.
- Transfer to buttered 2-quart baking dish and bake covered at 325° for 30 minutes.
- When ready to serve, sprinkle chopped green onion over top of casserole.

Squash Dressing

2 (6 ounce) packages Mexican cornbread mix
2 eggs
1 ⅓ cups milk
2 pounds yellow squash, sliced
1 cup water
½ cup (1 stick) margarine
1 cup chopped onion
1 cup chopped celery
½ cup chopped green bell pepper
1 (10 ounce) can cream of chicken soup, undiluted
2 teaspoons chicken bouillon

- Prepare cornbread according to package directions with eggs and milk. Cool and crumble into a large bowl.
- Combine squash and water in saucepan and bring to a boil. Cook about 10 minutes until squash is tender. Drain and mash.
- Melt margarine in skillet over medium heat and saute onion, celery and bell pepper.
- Combine crumbled cornbread, squash, onion mixture, cream of chicken soup and chicken bouillon. Mix well and spoon into greased 9 x 12-inch baking dish.
- Bake uncovered at 350° for 45 minutes.

Eggplant Frittata

3 cups peeled, finely chopped eggplant
½ cup chopped green bell pepper
3 tablespoons extra light olive oil
1 (8 ounce) jar roasted red peppers, drained, chopped
10 eggs
½ cup half-and-half-cream
¾ teaspoon salt
1 teaspoon seasoned salt
1 teaspoon Italian seasoning
¼ teaspoon pepper
⅓ cup grated parmesan cheese

- In skillet, cook eggplant and bell pepper in oil for 2 to 3 minutes, just until tender. Stir in roasted red peppers.
- In mixing bowl, combine eggs, cream, salt, seasoned salt, Italian seasoning and pepper and beat just until well blended.
- Add eggplant-pepper mixture to the egg-cream mixture. Pour into buttered 10-inch pie plate.
- Bake covered 325° for about 15 minutes or until center is set.
- Uncover and sprinkle parmesan cheese over top. Return to oven for about 5 minutes, just until cheese is slightly melted.
- Cut into wedges to serve.

This is a delicious eggplant for a light rich enough to be served course. You could put before the lunch, then way to serve lunch and it is as the main it together the day cook just before serving.

Creamy Macaroni
and Cheese

1 (12 ounce) package macaroni
6 tablespoons (¾ stick) margarine
¼ cup flour
2 cups milk
1 pound Velveeta cheese, cubed
1 teaspoon salt
½ teaspoon white pepper

- Cook macaroni according to package directions and drain.
- Melt margarine in saucepan and stir in flour until well blended.
- Slowly add milk stirring constantly and heat until it begins to thicken. Add cheese and stir until cheese melts.
- Pour cheese sauce over macaroni and mix well.
- Pour into buttered 2 ½-quart baking dish. Bake covered at 350° for 30 minutes or until bubbly.

Yes, this is more trouble than opening that "blue box", but it is well worth the time to make this macaroni and cheese.

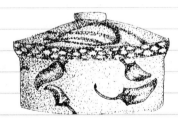

Unforgettable
Tortellini Bake

1 (18 ounce) package frozen cheese tortellini, cooked, drained
1 (16 ounce) package frozen chopped broccoli, thawed, drained
1 (4 ounce) jar diced pimentos
½ cup chopped onion
1 clove garlic, minced
2 tablespoons margarine
2 tablespoons flour
½ teaspoon salt
½ teaspoon seasoned salt
1 teaspoon Italian seasoning
¼ teaspoon white pepper
⅛ teaspoon ground nutmeg
1 cup half-and-half cream
⅓ cup grated parmesan cheese
½ cup shredded mozzarella cheese

- In large bowl, combine tortellini, broccolli and pimentos and set aside.
- In saucepan, saute onion and garlic in margarine. Over medium heat, stir in flour, salt, seasoned salt, Italian seasoning, pepper and nutmeg and mix well.
- Gradually stir in cream until well blended. Cook, stirring constantly, until sauce has thickened.
- Fold in parmesan cheese and stir until cheese melts. Fold in tortellini-broccoli mixture. Spoon into greased 2 ½-quart baking dish.
- Bake covered at 350° for 45 minutes or until hot and bubbly.
- Remove from oven and sprinkle mozzarella cheese over top of casserole. Return to oven for 5 minutes or until cheese melts.

Artichoke Squares

1 (6 ounce) jar marinated artichoke hearts, drained
1 (6 ounce) jar marinated artichoke hearts, reserve liquid
1 onion, finely chopped
½ teaspoon minced garlic
4 eggs, beaten
⅓ cup breadcrumbs
¼ teaspoon salt
¼ teaspoon white pepper
⅛ teaspoon oregano
⅛ teaspoon hot sauce
1 (8 ounce) package cheddar cheese
1 tablespoon dried parsley flakes

- Pour marinade from 1 jar of artichoke hearts in skillet, heat and saute onion and garlic.
- Chop artichokes from each jar and set aside.
- In a separate bowl, combine eggs, breadcrumbs, salt, pepper, oregano and hot sauce.
- Fold in cheese and parsley. Add artichokes and onions and mix well.
- Spoon into greased 9-inch square baking dish.
- Bake uncovered at 325° for 30 minutes. Allow several minutes before cutting into squares to serve.

These artichoke squares are perfect for a brunch because they can be served hot or at room temperature. They can also be made ahead of time and reheated when ready to serve.

Emerald Rice

2 (10 ounce) boxes frozen chopped spinach, thawed, well
drained
1 ½ cups cooked rice
1 (8 ounce) package shredded cheddar cheese
3 eggs, beaten
1 (5 ounce) can evaporated milk
3 tablespoons finely chopped onion
⅛ cup (¼ stick) butter, melted
1 teaspoon salt
1 teaspoon chicken bouillon
¼ teaspoon dried thyme
⅛ teaspoon ground nutmeg

- Cook spinach according to package directions and drain well.
- Stir in cooked rice and cheddar cheese.
- In separate bowl, combine eggs and evaporated milk and beat until well blended.
- Add onion, butter, salt, bouillon, thyme and nutmeg and mix well.
- Transfer to greased 2-quart casserole dish. Cover and bake at 350° for 20 minutes.
- Uncover and continue baking for another 20 minutes or until a knife inserted near the center comes out clean.

Not Just Buttered Rice

1 cup white rice, uncooked
1 ½ cups water
6 tablespoons (¾ stick) margarine, melted
1 teaspoon seasoned salt
½ teaspoon white pepper
1 teaspoon garlic powder
¼ cup dried parsley flakes
1 onion, finely chopped
1 egg, beaten
1 (16 ounce) box jalapeno processed cheese, cubed
1 cup milk

- In large bowl, combine rice, water, melted margarine, seasoned salt, pepper, garlic powder, parsley, onion and egg and mix well.
- In saucepan, combine cheese and milk and heat, stirring constantly, until cheese melts.
- Stir into rice-egg mixture. Spoon into a buttered 3-quart baking dish.
- Bake covered at 350° for 60 minutes. This can be cooked, frozen and reheated later.

A Different Stuffing

1 (6 ounce) package long grain, wild rice
¼ cup (½ stick) butter
1 ½ cups chopped celery
1 onion, chopped
1 sweet red bell pepper, finely chopped
1 small carrot, finely grated
¾ cup chopped walnuts
⅛ teaspoon cayenne pepper
1 (6 ounce) box chicken stuffing mix
1 egg
1 cup chicken broth

- Prepare rice according to directions.
- In a skillet, melt butter and saute celery, onion, bell pepper, carrot and walnuts. Stir in cayenne pepper.
- Prepare chicken stuffing according to directions.
- In a large bowl, combine rice, celery-carrot mixture, egg and prepared stuffing mix.
- Fold in broth and spoon into a buttered 3-quart baking dish.
- Cover and bake at 350° for 35 minutes.

Side Dishes

Red and Green Wild Rice

1 (6 ounce) package long grain, wild rice
1 sweet, red bell pepper, julienned
2 small zucchini, julienned
2 stalks fresh broccoli, cut into bite-size pieces
½ head cauliflower, cut into bite-size pieces
½ cup (1 stick) margarine, melted
1 teaspoon seasoned salt
1 teaspoon white pepper
1 teaspoon dried sweet basil
½ cup slivered almonds
1 (8 ounce) package shredded cheddar cheese

- Cook rice according to package directions and set aside,
- In large bowl, combine bell pepper, zucchini, broccoli and cauliflower. Cover with wax paper and microwave 3 minutes. Turn bowl and stir the vegetables. Microwave 2 more minutes.
- Add melted margarine, seasoned salt, pepper, basil, almonds and rice and toss together.
- Spoon into buttered 9 x 13-inch baking dish.
- Bake covered at 350° for about 20 minutes or until heated thoroughly.
- Just before serving, sprinkle cheese over top and return to oven for 5 minutes.

You have rice and vegetables all in one delicious dish - and besides that, you have color and character!

Creamy Rice Bake

1 cup finely chopped green onions and tops
¼ cup (½ stick) margarine
3 cups cooked instant white rice
1 (8 ounce) carton sour cream
¾ cup small curd cottage cheese
1 teaspoon seasoned salt
½ teaspoon white pepper
1 (4 ounce) can chopped green chilies, optional
1 ¼ cups monterey jack cheese
Paprika

- In large skillet, saute onion in margarine.
- Remove from heat and add rice, sour cream, cottage cheese, seasoned salt, pepper, green chilies and monterey jack cheese.
- Toss lightly to mix and spoon into a greased 2-quart baking dish.
- Bake covered at 350° for 35 minutes. Sprinkle lightly with paprika for garnish.

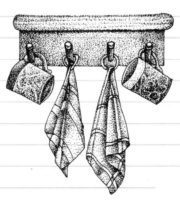

Italian Bake

1 pound Italian sausage links, sliced
3 cups fresh sliced mushrooms
1 onion, chopped
1 green bell pepper, chopped
1 teaspoon minced garlic
2 (15 ounce) cans Italian stewed tomatoes
1 teaspoon Italian seasoning
8 ounces rotini pasta, cooked al dente, drained
1 (8 ounce) package shredded mozzarella cheese, divided
1 (2 ounce) can pitted ripe olives, halved

- In large skillet, cook Italian sausage until slices are no longer pink, about 10 minutes. Remove sausage from skillet and reserve about 2 tablespoons of the drippings.
- In skillet, saute mushrooms, onions, bell pepper and garlic just until tender-crisp.
- In large bowl, combine sausage, mushroom-bell pepper mixture, stewed tomatoes, Italian seasoning, pasta and half of the mozzarella cheese and mix well.
- Spoon into greased 3-quart casserole dish. Cover and bake at 350° for 30 minutes.
- Remove from oven, sprinkle remaining cheese over top of casserole and return to oven for 5 minutes.
- When ready to serve, sprinkle olives over top of casserole.

A Special Rice

¾ cup pine nuts
3 tablespoons orange juice
1 cup dried currants
1 cup brown rice
1 cup white rice
2 tablespoons grated orange zest
2 tablespoon snipped parsley
4 tablespoons olive oil
1 teaspoon salt
½ teaspoon white pepper
1 (3 ounce) package grated parmesan cheese

- Spread out pine nuts over baking sheet and bake at 250° for 10 to 15 minutes, stirring once. Remove from oven and set aside.
- Pour orange juice over currants and set aside.
- Cook brown rice and white rice according to package directions and mix together in separate bowl.
- To rice mixture, add pine nuts, currants, orange zest, parsley, olive oil, salt and pepper. Mix thoroughly.
- Spoon mixture into sprayed baking dish, cover with foil and bake at 350° for 15 to 20 minutes until well heated.
- Sprinkle parmesan cheese and fresh parsley over top.

Festive Cranberries

2 (20 ounce) cans pie apples*
1 (16 ounce) can whole cranberries
¾ cup sugar
½ cup packed brown sugar

Topping:
¼ cup (½ stick) butter
1 ½ cups crushed corn flakes
⅔ cup sugar
½ teaspoon ground cinnamon
1 cup chopped pecans

- In bowl, combine pie apples, cranberries and both sugars and mix well. Spoon into buttered 2-quart baking dish.
- In saucepan, melt butter and mix in corn flakes, sugar, cinnamon and pecans.
- Sprinkle over apples and cranberries.
- Bake uncovered at 325° for 1 hour. This can be served hot or at room temperature.

Look for pie apples, not apple pie filling.

What a great dish for Thanksgiving or Christmas!

Early Morning
Vegetable Lasagna

1 (14 ½ ounce) can Italian-style stewed tomatoes
1 ½ cups pasta sauce
2 cups cottage cheese, drained
1 cup grated parmesan cheese
¼ teaspoon salt
¼ teaspoon white pepper
9 lasagna noodles, uncooked, divided
4 zucchini, shredded, divided
7 (1 ounce) provolone cheese slices, cut into strips, divided

- Stir together stewed tomatoes and pasta sauce and set aside.
- Stir together cottage cheese, parmesan cheese, salt and white pepper.
- Spoon one-third of tomato mixture into sprayed 9 x 13-inch baking dish.
- Place 3 uncooked lasagna noodles over tomato mixture and top with one-third of grated zucchini.
- Spoon one-third of cheese mixture over zucchini and top with one-third of provolone cheese strips.
- Repeat layering procedure twice. Cover and chill at least 8 hours.
- Remove from refrigerator and let stand for 30 minutes. Bake covered at 350° for 45 minutes.
- Uncover and bake additional 20 minutes. Let stand 15 minutes before serving.

This is "early morning" because it's so easy you can make it in the morning, go to work or play and it's ready to pop in the oven whenever you are ready. While it's chillin', you can be chillin' too.

Vegetable Casseroles

Sunshine On the Table

2 ½ cups finely shredded carrots
2 cups cooked rice
2 eggs, beaten
2 cups diced Velveeta cheese
1 (15 ounce) can cream-style corn
¼ cup half-and-half cream
2 tablespoons (¼ stick) margarine, melted
2 tablespoons dried minced onion
1 teaspoon seasoned salt
½ teaspoon white pepper

- In large bowl, combine all ingredients.
- Spoon into buttered 3-quart baking dish.
- Bake uncovered at 350° for 40 minutes or until set.

This is absolutely the prettiest casserole you will place on your table! And not only pretty, but it is also tasty, delicious, delectable, savory, appetizing, classic and elegant. Need I go on? You'll never want a simple, buttered carrot again!

Cheddar-Broccoli Bake

1 (10 ounce) can cheddar cheese soup
1 (8 ounce) package cheddar-jack cheese
⅓ cup milk
½ teaspoon seasoned salt
½ teaspoon white pepper
1 cup chopped celery
1 sweet red bell pepper, julienned
1 (16 ounce) bag frozen broccoli florets, cooked
1 can french-fried onion rings

- In a bowl, combine soup, cheese, milk, seasonings, celery, bell pepper and broccoli and mix well.
- Pour into buttered 3-quart casserole dish. Cover and bake at 325° for 25 minutes.
- Uncover, sprinkle onion rings over casserole and return to oven for 15 minutes or until onion rings are golden.

Broccoli Supreme

2 (10 ounce) packages broccoli spears
1 stick garlic cheese roll
1 (10 ounce) can cream of mushroom soup, undiluted
1 (3 ounce) can sliced mushrooms, drained
¾ cup seasoned breadcrumbs

- In a saucepan, boil broccoli for 3 minutes, drain. Place broccoli in a 2-quart baking dish.
- In another saucepan, combine cheese roll, soup and mushrooms. Heat on medium, stirring constantly until cheese melts.
- Spoon cheese-mushroom mixture over broccoli. Sprinkle breadcrumbs over top of casserole.
- Bake uncovered at 350° for 30 minutes.

Impossible Broccoli Pie

1 (16 ounce) package frozen broccoli spears, thawed
1 (12 ounce) package shredded cheddar cheese, divided
½ cup chopped onion
3 eggs, slightly beaten
¾ cup buttermilk biscuit mix
1 ½ cups milk
¾ teaspoon salt
¾ teaspoon pepper

- Cut large chunks of broccoli into smaller pieces and discard some of the stems.
- In large mixing bowl, combine broccoli, ⅔ of the cheese and all the onion and mix well. Spoon into greased 10-inch, deep-dish, pie plate.
- In the same mixing bowl, mix eggs and biscuit mix and beat for several minutes.
- Add milk, salt and pepper and mix until fairly smooth. Pour over broccoli and cheese mixture.
- Bake uncovered at 350° for 35 to 40 minutes or until knife inserted in center comes out clean.
- Top with remaining cheese and bake just until cheese melts. Let stand 5 minute before slicing to serve.

Broccoli is such a wonderful vegetable, so green, pretty and healthy too! There are so many ways to serve it: plain, buttered, loaded with cheeses, baked in souffle, creamed and crunchy good raw. It really perks up a salad and makes it special too.

Broccoli Souffle

4 cups fresh broccoli florets
2 tablespoons water
5 tablespoons margarine, melted
2 tablespoons flour
3 eggs, beaten
1 cup small curd cottage cheese, drained
½ cup half-and-half cream
1 cup shredded cheddar cheese, divided
½ cup minced onion
¼ teaspoon salt
½ teaspoon seasoned salt
½ teaspoon white pepper

- Cut broccoli into very small florets with very little stem. Place florets and water in a mircrowaveable bowl. Microwave on high for 3 minutes.
- Remove from microwave, add margarine, sprinkle flour over broccoli and toss.
- In bowl with beaten eggs, add cottage cheese, cream, ½ cup cheese, onion, salt, seasoned salt and white pepper and mix together well.
- Combine broccoli and egg mixture and pour into a buttered 7 x 11-inch baking dish or souffle dish. Sprinkle remaining ½ cup cheese over top.
- Bake uncovered at 350° for 30 to 35 minutes or until center is set.

Broccoli Frittata

3 tablespoons margarine
½ cup chopped onion
4 cups fresh broccoli florets without stems
6 large eggs
1 envelope cream of broccoli soup mix
½ cup shredded cheddar cheese
½ cup milk
½ teaspoon white pepper
½ teaspoon salt

- In skillet, melt margarine and saute onion. Add broccoli and 1 tablespoon water. Cook, stirring occasionally, on low heat for about 5 minutes until just tender crisp, but still bright green.
- In a separate bowl, whisk together eggs, soup mix, cheese, milk, pepper and salt. Fold in broccoli-onion mixture.
- Pour into buttered, 10-inch, deep dish pie pan.
- Bake at 350º for 20 to 25 minutes or until center is set.
- Let frittata set for 5 or 10 minutes before cutting into wedges to serve.

Broccoli-Rice Whiz

Vegetables

2 cups instant rice

¾ cup chopped onion

¾ cup chopped sweet red bell pepper

¾ cup chopped celery

¼ cup (½ stick) margarine

1 (8 ounce) jar Mexican processed cheese spread

1 (10 ounce) can cream of chicken soup, undiluted

½ cup whole milk

2 (10 ounce) packages frozen chopped broccoli, thawed, drained

- Cook rice in large saucepan.
- Saute onions, bell pepper and celery in margarine.
- Add onion-celery mixture to rice.
- Fold in cheese, chicken soup and milk and mix well.
- Heat on low until cheese and soup are well blended.
- Fold in chopped broccoli.
- Pour into a large greased 3-quart casserole and bake covered at 350° for 35 minutes.

So easy and so good! And it gives us a vegetable
and rice all in one dish.

Broccoli-Cauliflower Casserole

1 (10 ounce) box frozen broccoli florets, thawed
1 (10 ounce) box frozen cauliflower, thawed
1 egg, beaten
⅔ cup mayonnaise
1 (10 ounce) can cream of chicken soup, undiluted
¼ cup milk
1 onion, chopped
1 sweet red bell pepper, seeded, chopped
1 cup grated Swiss cheese
1 cup seasoned breadcrumbs
⅛ cup (¼ stick) margarine
Paprika

- Cook broccoli and cauliflower as directed on boxes. Drain well and place in a large mixing bowl.
- In a saucepan, combine egg, mayonnaise, soup, milk, onion, bell pepper and cheese and mix well. Heat just enough to be able to mix well.
- Spoon into mixing bowl with broccoli-cauliflower and mix well. Pour into a 2 ½-quart buttered baking dish.
- Combine breadcrumbs and margarine and sprinkle over broccoli and cauliflower mixture. Sprinkle paprika over top.
- Bake uncovered at 350° for 35 minutes.

Cauliflower Melody

1 head cauliflower, cut into florets
1 (15 ounce) can Italian stewed tomatoes, undrained
1 onion, finely chopped
1 green bell pepper, julienned
1 tablespoon sugar
1 teaspoon salt
½ teaspoon white pepper
1 tablespoon cornstarch
¼ cup (½ stick) margarine, melted
1 cup shredded cheddar cheese
1 cup Italian seasoned breadcrumbs

- Cook cauliflower in large saucepan with salted water for about 10 minutes or until tender-crisp and drain well.
- Combine stewed tomatoes, onion, bell pepper, sugar, salt, pepper, cornstarch and melted margarine and mix well.
- Transfer cauliflower and tomato mixture to 2-quart casserole dish and sprinkle cheese, then breadcrumbs over top.
- Bake uncovered at 350° for 35 minutes.

Baked Cauliflower

1 (16 ounce) package frozen cauliflower, thawed
1 egg
⅔ cup mayonnaise
1 (10 ounce) can cream of chicken soup
4 ounces Swiss cheese, grated
2 ribs celery, sliced
1 green bell pepper, chopped
1 onion, chopped
1 teaspoon white pepper
1 ½ cups round buttery cracker crumbs
Paprika

- Butter a 9 x 13-inch baking dish. Place cauliflower in dish and cover with plastic wrap leaving one corner open.
- Cook on high in microwave for 3 minutes. Turn dish and cook another 3 minutes on high.
- In medium saucepan, combine egg, mayonnaise, chicken soup and grated cheese. Heat just until well mixed.
- Add celery, bell pepper, onion and white pepper to cauliflower and mix well. Pour soup mixture over vegetables and spread out.
- Sprinkle cracker crumbs on top.
- Bake uncovered at 350° for 35 to 40 minutes or until cracker crumbs are light brown.
- Sprinkle paprika over top of casserole before serving.

Cauliflower Con Queso

1 large head cauliflower, broken into florets
¼ cup (½ stick) margarine
½ onion, chopped
2 tablespoons flour
1 (15 ounce) can Mexican-stewed tomatoes
1 (4 ounce) can chopped green chilies, drained
¾ teaspoon seasoned pepper
1 teaspoon salt
1 ½ cups shredded monterey jack cheese

- Cook cauliflower florets until just tender-crisp, drain and place in buttered 2-quart casserole dish.
- Melt margarine in medium saucepan. Saute onion just until clear and not browned.
- Blend in flour and stir in tomatoes. Cook, stirring constantly, until mixture thickens.
- Add green chilies, seasoned pepper and salt.
- Fold in cheese and stir until melted. Pour sauce over drained cauliflower.
- Cover and bake at 325° for about 15 minutes.

Cheese to the Rescue

1 large head cauliflower, cut into florets
1 sweet red bell pepper, julienned
½ cup chopped celery
½ cup (1 stick) butter, divided
1 (10 ounce) box frozen green peas, thawed
1 (8 ounce) package shredded Mexican 4-cheese blend,
divided
⅓ cup flour
1 teaspoon seasoned salt
½ teaspoon white pepper
1 pint half-and-half cream
½ cup milk

- In saucepan, cook cauliflower, covered in small amount of water until tender-crisp. Don't overcook.
- In small skillet, saute bell pepper and celery in 3 tablespoons butter.
- Add bell pepper, celery and peas to drained cauliflower and toss with half the cheese.
- Spoon into buttered 3-quart casserole dish.
- In another saucepan, combine remaining butter, flour, salt and pepper and mix well.
- On medium high heat gradually add cream and milk. Cook, stirring constantly, until mixture thickens. Pour over vegetables. Cover and bake at 325° for 20 minutes.
- Uncover and sprinkle remaining cheese over top of casserole. Return to oven for 5 minutes.

Crunchy Cauliflower and Friends

1 large head cauliflower, broken into florets
1 zucchini, cut in large pieces
1 sweet red bell pepper, julienned
1 (8 ounce) can whole kernel corn, drained
1 teaspoon seasoned salt
1 (8 ounce) carton sour cream
1 cup grated cheddar cheese
½ cup crushed corn flakes
¾ cup crushed buttery cracker crumbs
½ teaspoon salt
⅛ teaspoon cayenne pepper
⅓ cup grated parmesan cheese

- In large saucepan, combine cauliflower, zucchini and bell pepper, cover and cook in small amount of water for 5 to 7 minutes and drain.
- In large bowl, combine cauliflower-zucchini mixture, corn, seasoned salt, sour cream and cheddar cheese and mix just until sour cream and cheddar cheese coats vegetables.
- Combine corn flakes, cracker crumbs, salt and cayenne pepper.
- Sprinkle crumb mixture over vegetables and mix lightly just until vegetables are covered.
- Spoon vegetables into greased 9 x 13-inch baking dish. Sprinkle parmesan cheese over top of casserole.
- Bake uncovered at 325° for about 30 minutes or until crumbs are lightly browned.

Vegetables

Grand Cauliflower

¾ cup cooked, finely chopped ham
2 cloves garlic, finely minced
1 sweet red bell pepper, chopped
½ cup chopped onion
6 tablespoons (¾ stick) margarine, divided
1 (16 ounce) package frozen cauliflower, thawed
2 tablespoons flour
¾ teaspoon seasoned salt
½ teaspoon white pepper
1 ½ cups whipping cream
1 ½ cups shredded cheddar cheese
½ cup toasted, almond slivers
3 tablespoons minced fresh parsley

- In large skillet over medium heat, saute ham, garlic, red bell pepper and onion in 2 tablespoons margarine. Add cauliflower and 2 tablespoons water, cover and steam until tender-crisp.
- In separate skillet, melt remaining margarine. Add flour, salt and pepper and a little bit of the cream and stir well to blend.
- Add remaining cream, heat and cook, stirring constantly, until mixture thickens. Add cheese and stir.
- Spoon cauliflower-ham mixture into greased 2-quart baking dish. Pour cream mixture over the cauliflower. Sprinkle almonds on top of casserole.
- Cover and bake at 350° for 20 minutes, just until casserole is heated thoroughly.
- Remove from oven and sprinkle parsley and paprika over top.

Cauliflower may be cooked and buttered, dressed up with creamy white sauce, cheeses or perked up with Italian tomatoes. "Raw" will add flavor and crunch to any green salad. Cauliflower is a member of the cabbage family, but it beats cabbage by a mile. Mark Twain said "cauliflower is nothing but cabbage with a college education". Education is good!

Spinach Enchiladas

Vegetables

2 (10 ounce) boxes chopped spinach, thawed, pressed dry
1 envelope dry onion soup mix
3 cups shredded cheddar cheese, divided
3 cups shredded monterey jack cheese or mozzarella, divided
12 flour tortillas
1 pint whipping cream, unwhipped

- Use lots of paper towels to make sure the spinach is well drained.
- In medium bowl, combine spinach and onion soup mix. Blend in 1 ½ cups cheddar and 1 ½ cups jack cheeses.
- Spread out 12 tortillas and place about 3 heaping tablespoons of spinach mixture down middle of each tortilla and roll up.
- Place each filled tortilla, seam side down, into greased 10 x 14-inch baking dish.
- Pour whipping cream over enchiladas and sprinkle with remaining cheeses.
- Cover and bake at 350° for 20 minutes.
- Uncover and bake another 10 minutes longer.

Wow, are these good and this recipe will freeze well. To make ahead of time, freeze before adding the whipping cream and remaining cheeses. Thaw in the refrigerator before cooking. These enchiladas are great and so much fun to make and serve! Eat them all up because the tortillas got a little tough if reheated.

Spinach Delight

2 (10 ounce) boxes frozen, chopped spinach, thawed
1 (16 ounce) carton small curd cottage cheese
3 cups grated white cheddar cheese
4 eggs, beaten
3 tablespoons flour
¼ cup (½ stick) margarine, melted
½ teaspoon garlic salt
½ teaspoon celery salt
½ teaspoon lemon pepper
1 tablespoon dried onion flakes

- Drain spinach well by squeezing out liquid with several paper towels.
- In large bowl, mix together spinach, cottage cheese, cheddar cheese, eggs, flour, margarine, seasonings and onion flakes.
- Pour into buttered 2 ½-quart baking dish.
- Bake at 325° for 1 hour.

*This casserole may be made in advance
and baked when ready to serve.*

Spinach Special

3 (10 ounce) packages frozen chopped spinach
1 onion, chopped
½ cup (1 stick) butter
1 (8 ounce) package cream cheese, cubed
1 teaspoon seasoned salt
½ teaspoon white pepper
1 (14 ounce) can artichokes, drained, chopped
⅔ cup grated parmesan cheese

- In saucepan, cook spinach according to package directions, drain thoroughly and set aside.
- In skillet saute onion in butter, stir and cook until onion is clear but not browned.
- On low heat add cream cheese and stir constantly until cheese melts.
- Stir in spinach, seasonings and artichokes.
- Pour into a greased 2-quart baking dish. Sprinkle parmesan cheese over top of casserole.
- Cover and bake at 350° for 30 minutes.

Eat something green on New Year's Day to have money in the New Year. It's a great tradition and this is the dish to go with the tradition.

Easy Creamy Spinach

2 (10 ounce) packages frozen chopped spinach
1 (8 ounce) package cream cheese and chives, softened
⅔ cup shredded cheddar cheese
1 (10 ounce) can cream of celery soup
½ cup milk
1 egg, beaten
1 cup Cheez-It cracker crumbs

- In saucepan cook spinach according to package directions and drain.
- Add cream cheese and cheddar cheese to hot spinach, stir until both cheeses melt and mix well.
- Stir in soup, milk and egg and mix well.
- Pour into 2-quart buttered casserole dish. Top with cheese cracker crumbs.
- Bake uncovered for 350° for about 35 minutes.

Confetti-Squash Casserole

1 pound yellow squash, sliced
1 pound zucchini, sliced
1 large onion, chopped
¾ cup chopped green bell pepper
1 (10 ounce) can cream of chicken soup, undiluted
1 (8 ounce) carton sour cream
1 (4 ounce) jar chopped pimento, drained
1 (8 ounce) can sliced water chestnuts, drained
2 small carrots, grated
½ cup (1 stick) margarine
1 (6 ounce) box herb stuffing mix

- Cook squash, zucchini, onion and bell pepper in salted water for barely 10 minutes or until just tender crisp and drain well. (Be sure not to overcook.)
- In separate bowl, combine chicken soup, sour cream, pimento, water chestnuts and carrots and mix well.
- Melt margarine in large saucepan and add stuffing mix with its seasoning packet.
- Add squash-bell pepper mixture and soup-carrots mixture and mix gently, but well.
- Spoon into a buttered 3-quart baking dish.
- Bake uncovered at 325° for 35 minutes.

What a great vegetable dish and it is a very attractive dish as well!

Yummy Yellow Squash

4 cups sliced squash
1 onion, chopped
1 carrot, finely grated
1 (3 ounce) package cream cheese, softened, cubed
1 (4 ounce) jar chopped pimento, drained
1 (8 ounce) carton sour cream
1 cup small curd cottage cheese, drained
1 ½ cups monterey jack cheese
6 tablespoons (¾ stick) margarine, melted, divided
1 (6 ounce) package chicken-flavor stuffing mix, divided

- In large saucepan, cook squash, onion and grated carrot in a little salted water until tender-crisp. Drain.
- While mixture is still hot, fold in cream cheese and stir until cream cheese melts.
- Add pimento, sour cream, cottage cheese, monterey jack cheese and about 4 tablespoons melted margarine and mix well.
- Stir in half stuffing mix and all of seasoning package included with mix and fold into squash mixture. Spoon into lightly greased 3-quart baking dish.
- Sprinkle remaining stuffing over top and drizzle remaining melted margarine over top.
- Bake uncovered at 350° for 35 minutes.

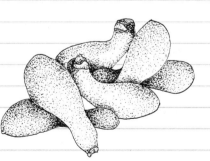

Posh Squash

3 pounds yellow squash, sliced
1 onion, chopped
1 (8 ounce) package grated Velveeta cheese
2 eggs, beaten
1 tablespoon sugar
1 (4 ounce) jar chopped pimento
1 teaspoon salt
1 teaspoon white pepper
6 tablespoons (¾ stick) margarine, melted

Topping:
2 cups cracker crumbs
¼ cup (½ stick) margarine, melted
1 (2.8 ounce) can fried onion rings

- In large saucepan, boil together squash and onion until tender. Drain and mash with a potato masher.
- Add cheese, stirring constantly, heat on low burner just until cheese melts. Add remaining ingredients, except topping, and blend well.
- Pour into buttered 9 x 13-inch baking dish.
- Mix crumbs and margarine and sprinkle over casserole.
- Bake uncovered at 350° for 35 minutes.
- Add fried onion rings to top and bake an additional 10 minutes.

Zucchini Bake

3 cups grated zucchini
1 ½ cups grated monterey jack cheese
4 eggs, beaten
½ teaspoon salt
¼ teaspoon garlic powder
½ teaspoon white pepper
2 cups cheese cracker crumbs

- In bowl, combine zucchini, cheese, eggs and seasoning and mix well. Spoon into buttered 2-quart baking dish.
- Sprinkle cracker crumbs over top.
- Bake uncovered at 350° for 35 to 40 minutes.

Zucchini is a popular summer squash that has a light and delicate flavor. When buying zucchini, select the smaller ones which will have a thinner skin. This delicious vegetable can be cooked many different ways or eaten raw in salads. Try adding sliced or chopped raw zucchini to your next green salad. You'll love the addition.

Zippy Zucchini

4 eggs
1 (8 ounce) package shredded monterey jack cheese
4 cups grated zucchini
1 (4 ounce) cup chopped green chilies
1 (4 ounce) jar sliced pimentos, drained
1 onion, finely minced
1 teaspoon creole seasoning
½ teaspoon white pepper
1 ½ cups crushed seasoned croutons
1 (3 ounce) package grated parmesan cheese

- In large mixing bowl, beat eggs well. Stir in cheese, zucchini, green chilies, pimentos, onion, creole seasoning and white pepper and mix well.
- Pour into well greased 2-quart baking dish.
- Bake uncovered at 350° for 35 minutes.
- Mix together crushed croutons and parmesan cheese and set aside.
- After 35 minutes of baking, sprinkle crouton mixture over casserole and bake another 10 minutes.

Zucchini on the Ritz

3 pounds zucchini, sliced
1 sweet, red bell pepper, finely diced
6 tablespoons (¾ stick) margarine
2 tablespoons flour
1 (5 ounce) can evaporated milk
¼ cup milk
1 (8 ounce) package grated Velveeta cheese
1 (4 ounce) can chopped green chilies
1 (4 ounce) jar chopped pimentos
1 teaspoon seasoned salt
½ teaspoon white pepper
2 ½ cups crushed butter crackers
⅓ cup slivered almonds

- In saucepan, boil zucchini and bell pepper just until barely tender but do not overcook.
- Make a white sauce by melting margarine in large saucepan and stir in flour, mixing well. Slowly add evaporated milk and milk and cook, stirring constantly on low heat, until white sauce is thick and smooth.
- Stir in cheese and heat just until cheese melts.
- Add chilies, pimentos, salt and pepper and fold in cooked, well-drained zucchini-bell pepper mixture.
- Pour into greased 3-quart baking dish and top with cracker crumbs.
- Sprinkle almonds over top of crumbs.
- Bake uncovered at 325° for 35 minutes or until hot and bubbly.

This delicious zucchini dish may be made the day before, but wait to add crumbs and almonds until you cook it.

Not-Your-Banquet Beans

3 (15 ounce) cans cut green beans, drained
1 (8 ounce) can sliced water chestnuts, drained, chopped
½ cup slivered almonds
½ cup chopped roasted, sweet red bell peppers
1 (16 ounce) box Mexican Velveeta cheese
1 ½ cups cracker crumbs
¼ cup (½ stick) margarine, melted

- Place green beans in buttered 9 x 13-inch baking dish and cover with water chestnuts, almonds and roasted, red bell pepper.
- Cut Velveeta cheese into small cubes and spread them over green bean-almond mixture.
- Place casserole in microwave and heat just barely enough for cheese to begin to melt. (Watch closely.)
- Combine cracker crumbs and margarine and sprinkle over casserole.
- Bake uncovered at 350° for 30 minutes.

You didn't really want plain green beans, did you?

Fancy Green Bean Bake

2 (16 ounce) packages frozen French-style green beans,
thawed
½ cup (1 stick) butter
1 (8 ounce) package fresh mushrooms, sliced
1 onion, chopped
¼ cup flour
1 pint half-and-half cream
1 cup milk
½ cup chopped, roasted red bell peppers
2 teaspoons soy sauce
1 teaspoon seasoned salt
½ teaspoon seasoned pepper
1 cup shredded cheddar cheese
⅔ cup chopped cashew nuts
½ cup chow mein noodles

- Cook green beans according to package directions, drain and set aside.
- In large saucepan, melt butter and saute mushrooms and chopped onion. Stir in flour and cook on medium heat for 1 minute, stirring constantly.
- Gradually add cream and milk stirring until well blended.
- Add red peppers, soy sauce, salt, pepper and cheese, stirring constantly, until cheese melts and mixture is thick.
- Combine sauce and green beans and pour into greased 9 x 13-inch baking dish.
- Combine cashews and chow mein noodles and sprinkle over top of casserole.
- Bake uncovered at 325° for 30 minutes.

Green Bean Supreme

2 tablespoons (¼ stick) margarine
1 (10 ounce) can cream of mushroom soup, undiluted
1 (3 ounce) package cream cheese, softened
3 (15 ounce) cans French-style green beans, drained
1 tablespoon dried onion flakes
1 (8 ounce) can sliced water chestnuts, drained
½ teaspoon garlic powder
½ teaspoon seasoned salt
1 ½ cups shredded cheddar cheese
1 ½ cups cracker crumbs
½ cup slivered almonds

- Melt margarine in large saucepan and add soup and cream cheese. Cook over low heat, stirring constantly, just until cream cheese melts and mixture is fairly smooth.
- Remove from heat and stir in green beans, onion flakes, water chestnuts, garlic powder, seasoned salt and cheese. Mix well.
- Pour into buttered 9 x 13-inch casserole dish. Top with cracker crumbs and then sprinkle with almonds.
- Bake uncovered at 350° for 30 minutes or until casserole bubbles around edges.

Bundles of Green

3 (15 ounce) cans whole green beans, drained
1 pound bacon
2 (15 ounce) cans new potatoes, drained
2 (10 ounce) cans fiesta nacho cheese soup
1 ½ cups milk

- Place 6 to 7 whole green beans together in a bundle, wrap with ½ strip of bacon and secure with toothpicks.
- Place bundles in large baking dish so bundles do not touch each other. Place under broiler in oven until bacon is cooked on both sides. Turn once while bacon is cooking.
- Spoon off bacon drippings and place potatoes around bundles.
- In saucepan combine nacho cheese soup and milk and heat just enough to mix well. Pour over green beans and potatoes.
- Cover and bake at 350° for 20 minutes or just until sauce is bubbly.

Green Bean Delight

Vegetables

¼ cup (4 tablespoons) margarine, divided
½ cup chopped onion
½ cup chopped celery
1 tablespoon flour
1 teaspoon sugar
¾ teaspoon seasoned salt
¼ teaspoon white pepper
1 cup half-and-half cream
3 (15 ounce) cans French-style green beans, drained
¾ cup crushed cornflakes
1 cup shredded Swiss cheese

- Melt 2 tablespoons margarine in skillet and saute onion and celery. Stir in flour, sugar, salt and pepper. Cook 1 minute on medium heat, stirring constantly.
- Reduce heat and slowly add cream and stir until smooth. Cook and stir over low heat for about 2 minutes until mixture is thick, but do not boil.
- Fold in green beans. Spread into greased 9 x13-inch baking dish.
- Melt remaining margarine and toss with cornflake crumbs, mix in cheese and sprinkle over top of casserole.
- Bake uncovered at 325° for about 25 minutes or until heated thoroughly.

Deluxe Green Beans

2 (15 ounce) cans French-style green beans, drained
1 (10 ounce) can cream of chicken soup, undiluted
1 (15 ounce) can shoepeg corn, drained
1 onion, chopped
1 sweet red bell pepper, chopped
1 cup finely chopped celery
1 (8 ounce) can sliced water chestnuts, drained
1 (8 ounce) carton sour cream
1 cup grated Velveeta cheese
3 tablespoons margarine
1 cup crushed butter-flavored crackers
⅓ cup slivered almonds

- In large bowl, combine green beans, soup, corn, onion, bell pepper, celery, water chestnuts, sour cream and cheese and mix well. Transfer to greased 9 x 13-inch baking dish.
- In skillet, melt margarine and add cracker crumbs and almonds. Cook over low heat and stir until lightly browned. Sprinkle over top of casserole.
- Bake uncovered at 350° for 45 minutes or until topping is golden brown.

Beans and More Beans

½ pound bacon

2 large onions, chopped

1 cup chopped celery

1 cup chopped green bell pepper

1 ½ cups packed brown sugar

⅓ cup cider vinegar

1 tablespoon prepared mustard

1 teaspoon seasoned salt

1 (15 ounce) can kidney beans, rinsed, drained

1 (15 ounce) can navy beans, rinsed, drained

1 (15 ounce) can lima beans, rinsed, drained

1 (15 ounce) can pork and beans, undrained

1 (15 ounce) can pinto beans, drained

- In large skillet, cook bacon until crisp and drain.
- With bacon drippings remaining in skillet, saute onions, celery and bell pepper. Add brown sugar, vinegar, mustard and seasoned salt.
- In large bowl combine onion, bell pepper, bacon and all the beans. Pour into buttered 4-quart casserole dish.
- Cover and bake at 325° for 2 hours.

Country Baked Beans

4 (15 ounce) cans baked beans, drained
1 (8 ounce) bottle chili sauce
1 onion, chopped
½ pound bacon, cooked, crumbled
2 cups packed brown sugar

- In ungreased 3-quart baking dish, combine all ingredients. Stir until well blended.
- Bake uncovered at 325° for 55 minutes or until bubbly around edges.

Corn-Zucchini Success

Vegetables

3 unpeeled zucchini
½ cup chopped green bell peppers
½ cup chopped red bell pepper
½ cup chopped onion
5 tablespoons margarine, divided
¼ cup flour
½ teaspoon seasoned salt
1 teaspoon white pepper
1 (15 ounce) can cream-style corn
1 (3 ounce) package cream cheese, cubed
⅔ cup grated Swiss cheese
1 (15 ounce) can whole kernel corn, drained
½ cup chopped pecans
1 cup seasoned breadcrumbs

- Grate zucchini, drain well on paper towels and set aside.
- In saucepan, saute bell peppers and onion in 2 tablespoons margarine. Add remaining margarine, flour, salt and pepper and mix well.
- On medium-high heat, add cream-style corn, stirring constantly until mixture thickens.
- Add pepper-onion mixture, cream cheese and Swiss cheese and heat on low until cheeses melt.
- Add whole kernel corn, zucchini and pecans and mix well. Spoon into buttered 2-quart baking dish.
- Sprinkle breadcrumbs over top of casserole.
- Bake uncovered at 350° for 30 minutes or until breadcrumbs are lightly browned.

Corn With An Attitude

1 (15 ounce) can whole kernel corn
1 (15 ounce) can cream-style corn
½ cup (1 stick) margarine, melted
2 eggs, beaten
1 (8 ounce) carton sour cream
1 (6 ounce) package jalapeno cornbread mix
½ cup shredded cheddar cheese

- Mix all ingredients, except cheese in large bowl.
- Pour into buttered 9 x 13-inch baking dish.
- Bake uncovered at 350° for 35 minutes.
- Uncover and sprinkle cheese on top of casserole. Return to oven for 5 minutes.

You will always find this corn casserole or a
very similar version at church suppers.
And the dish will always be empty at the end of the evening.

Kid-Pleasing Corn

3 eggs, beaten
1 (8 ounce) carton sour cream
½ cup yellow cornmeal
½ cup (1 stick) margarine, melted
1 (8 ounce) can cream-style corn
1 (15 ounce) can whole kernel yellow corn, drained
1 (8 ounce) package shredded cheddar-jack cheese
½ teaspoon celery salt
1 teaspoon seasoned salt
¼ teaspoon white pepper

- In bowl, combine all ingredients and mix well. Pour into a greased 2-quart baking dish.
- Bake uncovered at 350° for 45 minutes or until center is set. Let stand 5 minutes before serving.

Fiesta Corn

1 (15 ounce) can cream-style corn
1 (15 ounce) can whole kernel corn, drained
1 bell pepper, seeded, chopped
1 onion, chopped
1 (4 ounce) can chopped green chilies
2 tablespoons (¼ stick) margarine, melted
2 eggs beaten
1 teaspoon sugar
¾ teaspoon seasoned salt
½ teaspoon seasoned pepper
⅛ teaspoon cayenne pepper
1 ½ cups buttery cracker crumbs, divided
1 cup shredded 4-cheese blend

Topping:
2 tablespoons grated parmesan cheese
Paprika for garnish

- In large mixing bowl, mix well both cans of corn, bell pepper, onion, green chilies, margarine, eggs, sugar, salt, pepper, cayenne pepper, ½ cup cracker crumbs and cheese.
- Pour into buttered 9 x 13-inch baking dish.
- Combine remaining 1 cup cracker crumbs and parmesan cheese and sprinkle over casserole.
- Bake uncovered at 350° for 45 minutes.
- Garnish with a few sprinkles of paprika.

Scalloped Corn
and Tomatoes

Vegetables

2 (15 ounce) cans Mexican-stewed tomatoes, undrained
2 (15 ounce) cans whole kernel corn, drained
½ cup (1 stick) margarine, melted, divided
1 (8 ounce) package shredded cheddar cheese
1 onion, chopped
2 tablespoons cornstarch
2 eggs, beaten
2 teaspoons sugar
½ teaspoon salt
½ teaspoon seasoned salt
1 teaspoon white pepper
½ teaspoon garlic powder
1 ½ cups round buttery cracker crumb

- In large bowl, mix together tomatoes, corn, 6 tablespoons (¾ stick) margarine, cheese, onion, cornstarch, eggs, sugar and seasonings. Pour into buttered 9 x 13-inch baking dish.
- Bake uncovered at 350° for 35 minutes.
- In small bowl, mix crumbs and 2 tablespoons (¼ stick) margarine. Sprinkle over top of casserole.
- Bake uncovered for 15 minutes more.

Asparagus Bake

4 (10.5 ounce) cans whole asparagus, drained
3 eggs, hard-boiled, sliced
2 tablespoons (¼ stick) butter, melted
⅓ cup milk
1 ½ cups shredded cheddar cheese
1 ¼ cups cheese cracker crumbs

- Place asparagus in buttered 7 x 11-inch baking dish. Arrange hard-boiled eggs on top and drizzle with butter.
- Pour milk over casserole.
- Sprinkle cheese on top, then add cracker crumbs.
- Bake uncovered at 350° for 30 minutes.

Swiss Asparagus

3 (15 ounce) cans asparagus spears, drained
1 ½ cups sour cream
½ cup shredded Swiss cheese
2 tablespoons dried minced onion flakes
¾ teaspoon seasoned salt
¼ teaspoon white pepper
¼ teaspoon dry mustard
¼ teaspoon garlic powder
1 cup fresh breadcrumbs
3 tablespoons margarine, melted

- Place asparagus in 1 ½-quart buttered casserole dish.
- Combine sour cream, Swiss cheese, onion flakes, salt, pepper, dry mustard and garlic powder and mix well to blend.
- Spoon sour cream mixture over asparagus.
- Toss breadcrumbs with melted margarine and sprinkle over casserole.
- Bake uncovered at 325° for 30 minutes.

Asparagus-Cheese Bake

3 (15 ounce) cans cut asparagus spears, reserve liquid
3 hard-boiled eggs, chopped
½ cup chopped pecans
1 (10 ounce) can cream of asparagus soup, undiluted
¼ cup (½ stick) margarine
½ teaspoon white pepper
2 cups cracker crumbs
1 (8 ounce) package shredded monterey jack cheese

- Arrange drained asparagus spears in buttered 2-quart casserole dish. Top with chopped eggs and pecans.
- Heat asparagus soup, reserved liquid from asparagus, margarine and pepper. Pour over asparagus, eggs and pecans.
- Combine cracker crumbs and cheese. Sprinkle over casserole.
- Bake uncovered at 350° for 25 minutes.

Baked Tomatoes

2 (15 ounce) cans diced tomatoes, drained
1 ½ cups toasted breadcrumbs, divided
Scant ¼ cup sugar
½ teaspoon salt
½ onion, chopped
¼ cup (½ stick) margarine, melted

- Combine tomatoes, 1 cup breadcrumbs, sugar, salt, onion and margarine.
- Pour into 2-quart buttered baking dish and cover with remaining breadcrumbs.
- Bake uncovered at 325°.

This is a really old recipe, but well worth reviving. People who had gardens always had plenty of tomatoes and this was their way of making a hot dish with tomatoes. Try it - you'll like it!

Vegetables

Black-Eyed Peas and Tomatoes

1 bell pepper, seeded, chopped
1 large onion, chopped
2 ribs celery, chopped
2 tablespoons (¼ stick) margarine
2 (15 ounce) can jalapeno black-eyed peas, drained
1 (15 ounce) can stewed tomatoes, undrained
1 teaspoon garlic powder
¼ cup ketchup
2 teaspoons dry chicken bouillon

- Saute bell pepper, onion and celery in margarine to tender-crisp, but do not overcook.
- In bowl, combine pepper-celery mixture, black-eyed peas, stewed tomatoes, garlic powder, ketchup and chicken bouillon. Spoon into 2-quart casserole dish.
- Cover and bake at 350° for about 20 minutes or just until bubbly.

This dish is a "must" for Southerners on New Year's Day because eating black-eyed peas will bring good luck for the coming year!

Crispy Gingered Peas

2 (10 ounce) packages frozen peas

3 tablespoons margarine

1 (6 ounce) can sliced mushrooms, drained

1 (8 ounce) can sliced water chestnuts, drained

1 bunch green onions, chopped

1 (4 ounce) jar chopped pimento, drained

¾ teaspoon ground ginger

¼ teaspoon nutmeg

1 (14 ounce) can chicken broth, divided

2 tablespoons cornstarch

½ teaspoon salt

¼ teaspoon garlic powder

3 tablespoons finely chopped crystallized ginger

- In large saucepan, place peas, margarine, mushrooms, water chestnuts, green onions, pimento, ginger, nutmeg and all but ¼ cup chicken broth. Cover and simmer over low heat for 6 to 8 minutes.
- In a cup, blend cornstarch and reserved chicken broth until smooth. Stir into peas-mushroom mixture.
- Cook slowly, stirring constantly, until liquid boils and thickens.
- Add salt, garlic powder and crystallized ginger and mix well.
- Pour into buttered 2-quart baking dish and bake covered at 325° for 20 minutes.

Crackered Onion Casserole

3 cups round buttery cracker crumbs
½ cup (1 stick) margarine, melted, divided
2 onions, thinly sliced

Sauce:
1 cup milk
2 eggs, slightly beaten
1 teaspoon seasoned salt
½ teaspoon white pepper
1 (8 ounce) package shredded cheddar cheese

- Combine and mix cracker crumbs and half the melted margarine. Place in 9 x 13-inch baking dish and pat down.
- Saute onions in remaining margarine. Spread onions over crust.
- For the sauce, combine milk, eggs, seasoned salt, pepper and cheese in saucepan. Heat on low just until cheese melts. Pour sauce over onions
- Bake uncovered at 300° for 45 minutes or until knife inserted in center comes out clean.

Serve as a replacement for potatoes or rice.

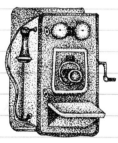

Smiling Onions

6 onions, sliced
1 sweet red bell pepper, julienne
½ cup (1 stick) butter, divided
1 (10 ounce) box frozen green peas, thawed
1 cup slivered almonds, toasted
1 tablespoon cornstarch
1 teaspoon seasoned salt
1 teaspoon white pepper
1 ½ cups half-and-half cream
½ cup grated parmesan cheese
5 strips bacon, cooked, crumbled

- In large skillet, on low heat, saute onions and bell pepper in ¼ cup (½ stick) butter, but do not let onions brown. Add peas and almonds.
- In saucepan, melt ¼ cup (½ stick) butter, add cornstarch, salt and pepper and stir until smooth. Gradually stir in cream and parmesan cheese and cook, stirring constantly, until sauce thickens.
- Pour over onion mixture. Spoon into buttered 3-quart baking dish.
- Cover and bake at 350° for 30 minutes.
- Remove from oven and sprinkle crumbled bacon over top of casserole.

Mushroom-Onion Pie

1 large onion, halved, thinly sliced
2 cups fresh mushroom, sliced
1 tablespoon olive oil
4 eggs, slightly beaten
1 (8 ounce) carton whipping cream
½ teaspoon thyme
½ teaspoon basil
1 ½ teaspoons salt
1 teaspoon white pepper
⅛ teaspoon ground nutmeg
1 (9 inch) frozen deep-pastry shell, thawed

- Saute onion slices and mushrooms in oil and cook on low heat for about 10 minutes, but do not brown.
- In bowl, combine eggs, whipping cream, thyme, basil, salt, white pepper and nutmeg and mix well. Pour into onion-mushroom mixture and stir.
- Place pastry shell on baking sheet and spoon in all ingredients.
- Bake uncovered at 350° for 45 minutes or until center is set.

Creamy Vegetable Casserole

1 (16 ounce) package frozen broccoli, carrots and cauliflower
1 (10 ounce) box frozen green peas
1 (10 ounce) can cream of mushroom soup, undiluted
½ cup milk
1 (8 ounce) carton spreadable garden vegetable cream
cheese
1 cup seasoned, crushed croutons

- Cook all vegetables according to package directions, but don't overcook! Drain and place in large bowl.
- In saucepan, place soup, milk and cream cheese and heat just enough to mix easily.
- Pour into vegetable mixture and stir well.
- Spoon into 2-quart baking dish. Sprinkle with croutons.
- Bake uncovered at 350° for 25 minutes or until bubbly.

These are vegetables at their best!

Vegetables

Absolutely Delicious Vegetables

2 (15 ounce) cans mixed vegetables, drained
1 cup chopped celery
½ onion, chopped
1 (8 ounce) can sliced water chestnuts, drained
1 cup shredded sharp cheddar cheese
¾ cup mayonnaise
1 ½ cups round buttery crackers, crushed
6 tablespoons (¾ stick) margarine, melted

- In bowl, combine vegetables, celery, onion, water chestnuts, cheese and mayonnaise and mix well. Spoon into buttered 9 x 13-inch baking dish.
- Combine crushed crackers and melted margarine and sprinkle over vegetable mixture.
- Bake at 350° for 30 minutes or until crackers are lightly browned.

You will just have to make this dish to know how really good this recipe is. A friend at church started making this years ago and she always gets requests for these vegetables. Amazingly, you don't realize that it is loaded with vegetables. (What a great way to get your kids to eat vegetables!) The crispy top just sets it off and it couldn't be easier!

Vegetable Frittata

4 tablespoons light olive oil
1 onion, chopped
¾ cup chopped green bell pepper
¾ cup chopped sweet red bell pepper
2 cups chopped zucchini
2 cups chopped yellow squash
¼ cup half-and-half cream
1 (8 ounce) package cream cheese, softened
6 eggs
1 cup shredded mozzarella cheese
¾ teaspoon garlic powder
¾ teaspoon seasoned salt
½ teaspoon white pepper
2 teaspoons white wine worcestershire sauce
1 cup seasoned breadcrumbs
3 tablespoons butter, melted

- Heat oil in large skillet. Saute onion, bell peppers, zucchini and squash just until tender-crisp. Remove from heat and set aside to cool.
- In mixing bowl, beat together half-and-half with cream cheese until creamy. Add eggs and beat about 4 minutes until both are well mixed.
- Add mozzarella cheese, seasonings and white wine worcestershire and mix by hand. (Do not use dark worcestershire because it makes vegetables too dark.)
- Fold in breadcrumbs, melted butter and vegetables. Pour into greased 9-inch springform pan.
- Bake uncovered at 350° for 55 to 60 minutes or until lightly browned and set in center.
- Set aside for 10 minutes before slicing to serve. (Be sure to use a thin, sharp knife to cut around the edge of the springform pan before you open the pan.)

This makes an elegant dish and is perfect for a brunch or late supper.

The Veggie Patch

1 (10 ounce) can cream of chicken soup, undiluted
1 (10 ounce) can cream of celery soup, undiluted
½ cup milk
1 ½ cups shredded cheddar cheese
1 teaspoon seasoned salt
1 teaspoon dried basil
1 teaspoon white pepper
1 (8 ounce) can whole kernel corn, drained
1 (16 ounce) package frozen broccoli florets, thawed
1 (16 ounce) package frozen cauliflower, thawed
1 sweet red bell pepper, julienned
1 green bell pepper, julienned
1 ½ cups round butter cracker crumbs
2 tablespoons margarine, melted

- In saucepan, combine soups, milk, cheese, salt, basil and white pepper and heat just enough to pour.
- In buttered 3-quart casserole dish, combine corn, broccoli (cut some of the stems off and discard), cauliflower and bell peppers.
- Pour soup-cheese mixture over vegetables. Sprinkle buttered cracker crumbs over casserole.
- Bake uncovered at 325° for about 35 minutes.

Have you got a slice of ham? Well, that's all you need to serve with these wonderfully seasoned vegetables to make a great meal.

Spicy Vegetable Couscous

1 (5.7 ounce) package herbed chicken couscous
3 tablespoons margarine
3 tablespoons oil
1 small yellow squash, diced
1 small zucchini, diced
½ red onion, diced
1 sweet red bell pepper, diced
1 (10 ounce) box frozen green peas, thawed
½ teaspoon garlic powder
½ teaspoon ground cumin
½ teaspoon curry powder
¼ teaspoon red or cayenne pepper
½ teaspoon salt
1 ½ cups shredded mozzarella cheese

- Cook couscous according to package directions, but add 3 tablespoons margarine instead of amount specified.
- In large skillet, heat oil and saute squash, zucchini, onion and bell pepper for about 10 minutes; do not brown. Add peas, garlic powder, cumin, curry powder, red pepper and salt and toss.
- Combine vegetables and couscous. If it seems a little dry, add a few tablespoons water.
- Pour into buttered 2 ½-quart baking dish and sprinkle with mozzarella cheese.
- Bake covered at 350° for about 25 minutes.

This is not only really good, but is also a very colorful and attractive dish. This may be refrigerated and heated later. Allow it to sit at room temperature for about 30 minutes before heating.
If you prefer a milder hot, use only ⅛ teaspoon red pepper.

Summer Pie

3 large tomatoes, peeled, sliced
½ teaspoon salt
1 (9-inch) deep-dish frozen pie crust, thawed
4 bacon slices, cooked, drained, crumbled
1 tablespoon bacon drippings, reserved
3 yellow onions, halved, thinly sliced
1 cup shredded cheddar cheese
1 cup mayonnaise
½ teaspoon white pepper
1 (3 ounce) package grated parmesan cheese
2 tablespoons seasoned breadcrumbs

- Place tomatoes on paper towels and sprinkle with ½ teaspoon salt. Let stand 30 minutes.
- Place pie crust in deep dish pie plate and crimp edges of crust.
- Bake at 400° for about 10 minutes or until lightly browned.
- In large skillet, saute onions in bacon drippings. Spoon onions over prepared pie crust and top with tomato slices.
- In bowl, combine cheese, mayonnaise and pepper. Spread mixture over tomato slices.
- Combine parmesan cheese and breadcrumbs and sprinkle over top.
- Bake at 350° for 30 minutes or until lightly brown.
- Sprinkle crumbled bacon over top of pie.
- Let stand 5 minutes before serving.

Awesome Butternut Casserole

2 ½ cups cooked, mashed butternut squash
6 tablespoons (¾ stick) margarine, melted
¾ cup sugar
3 tablespoons brown sugar
3 eggs, beaten
1 (5 ounce) can evaporated milk
1 teaspoon vanilla
½ teaspoon cinnamon

Topping:
1 cups crushed corn flakes
½ cup packed light brown sugar
½ cup chopped pecans
2 tablespoons (¼ stick) margarine, melted

- (The best way to cook a butternut squash is to cut the squash in half, scoop out seeds and membranes and place cut-side down on plate and microwave on high for 1 to 2 minutes. Let stand in microwave for several minutes. Try to scoop out meat of squash. If it is not soft enough, microwave another minute.)
- Place scooped-out squash in mixing bowl and beat until fairly smooth.
- Place 2 ½ cups mashed squash (discard extra squash) in a large bowl. Add margarine, sugar, brown sugar, eggs, milk, vanilla and cinnamon and mix well. (Mixture will be thin.)
- Pour into buttered 3-quart baking dish.
- Bake uncovered at 350° for 45 minutes or until almost set.
- Combine topping ingredients and sprinkle over hot casserole and return to oven for 10 to 15 minutes or until top is crunchy.

This is really a wonderful fall dish. Of course it is a challenge to tackle the butternut squash, but it is worth the effort and you will be so pleased with the results!

Wraps Italienne

1 (10 ounce) box frozen chopped spinach, thawed
1 (8 ounce) can whole kernel corn, drained
1 (15 ounce) carton ricotta cheese
1 egg
2 (8 ounce) packages fancy shredded Italian cheese blend,
divided
8 flour tortillas
1 (15 ounce) can Italian-style stewed tomatoes, undrained
1 (8 ounce) can tomato sauce
1 teaspoon Italian seasoning
1 teaspoon salt
1 teaspoon dried basil
1 (3 ounce) package grated parmesan cheese

- Press spinach into several paper towels to drain. Repeat to make sure spinach is well drained.
- In medium bowl, combine spinach, corn, ricotta cheese, egg and 1 (8 ounce) package shredded Italian cheese blend and mix well.
- Lay all tortillas out on counter and place a heaping ¼ cup of this mixture in center of each tortilla.
- Roll up tightly and arrange seam-side down in greased 9 x 13-inch baking pan. Using the same bowl, combine stewed tomatoes, tomato sauce, Italian seasoning, salt and basil. Spoon mixture over the tortillas.
- Sprinkle with remaining Italian cheese.
- Bake uncovered at 350° for 30 minutes.
- Remove from oven and sprinkle parmesan cheese over top and return to oven for 5 minutes or just until parmesan melts.

*This is a fun dish to serve family or friends
and goes with most meals.*

Scalloped Potatoes

6 potatoes
½ cup (1 stick) margarine
White pepper
1 tablespoon flour
¾ cup milk
1 (8 ounce) package shredded cheddar cheese

- Peel and wash potatoes. Slice half of potatoes and place in 3-quart greased baking dish.
- Slice margarine and place half over potatoes.
- Sprinkle with pepper and flour.
- Slice remaining potatoes and place over first layer, add remaining margarine slices and pour milk over casserole.
- Sprinkle with a little more pepper and cover with cheese.
- Cover and bake at 350° for one hour. This must be cooked immediately or potatoes will darken. It can be frozen after baking and then reheated.

The Ultimate Potato

6 large baking potatoes, boiled
1 cup light cream
6 tablespoons (¾ stick) margarine
1 (8 ounce) package shredded cheddar cheese
1 (8 ounce) carton sour cream
1 teaspoon salt
1 teaspoon white pepper
½ cup chopped green onions
6 strips bacon, fried, crumbled

- Peel cooled potatoes and grate.
- Combine cream, margarine, cheese and sour cream in double boiler and stir just until melted.
- Add cheese mixture to grated potatoes and place in greased 3 to 4-quart baking dish.
- Cover and bake at 350° for 30 minutes.
- To serve, top with onions and crumbled bacon.

This is no time to count calories!

Glory Potatoes

1 (22 ounce) package frozen tater tots
2 eggs, beaten
1 (10 ounce) can cream of potato soup
1 (10 ounce) can cream of chicken soup
1 (8 ounce) carton sour cream
¾ cup milk
1 teaspoon salt
1 teaspoon seasoned salt
1 teaspoon white pepper
½ teaspoon garlic powder
1 sweet red bell pepper, julienned
1 green bell pepper, julienned
1 onion, chopped
1 (12 ounce) package shredded cheddar cheese, divided

- Butter 11 x 14-inch baking dish and arrange tater tots in bottom of casserole.
- In large bowl, combine eggs, both soups, sour cream, milk, seasonings, both bell peppers and onion and mix well.
- Fold in half the cheddar cheese. Spoon mixture over tater tots.
- Bake covered at 350° for 50 minutes or until bubbly.
- Remove from oven and sprinkle remaining cheese over casserole and return to oven for about 5 minutes.

Talk about a "good" potato, this is it!
And you don't have to peal a single potato.

New Potatoes
and Herb Butter

1 ½ pounds new potatoes
⅛ cup (¼ stick) butter, sliced
¼ teaspoon thyme
½ cup chopped fresh parsley
½ teaspoon rosemary

- Scrub potatoes and cut in halves unpeeled.
- In medium saucepan, boil potatoes in lightly salted water. Cook until potatoes are tender, about 15 minutes. Drain.
- Add butter, thyme, parsley and rosemary. Toss gently until butter is melted.

Did you know that, on average, an American eats 124 pounds of potatoes per year?

Hallelujah Potatoes

6 baking potatoes
½ cup (1 stick) butter
1 teaspoon salt
1 teaspoon pepper
1 (8 ounce) package cream cheese, softened
1 bunch fresh green onions and tops, sliced
1 (6 ounce) can crabmeat, drained, flaked
1 cup shredded cheddar cheese

- Bake potatoes at 400° for 1 hour or until done.
- Halve potatoes lengthwise and scoop out pulp, reserving skins.
- In mixing bowl, beat together hot potatoes, butter, salt, pepper and cream cheese and beat well. Stir in onions and crabmeat.
- Fill reserved skins with potato mixture. Sprinkle cheese over top of potatoes.
- Place on baking sheet and bake at 350° for 20 minutes or until bubbly hot.

How can you beat a "super" baked potato?

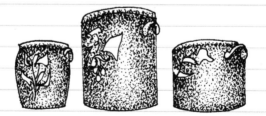

Cheddar-Potato Casserole

1 (2 pound) bag frozen hash brown potatoes, thawed
1 onion, finely chopped
½ cup (1 stick) margarine, melted
1 (8 ounce) carton sour cream
1 (10 ounce) can cream of chicken soup
1 (8 ounce) package shredded cheddar cheese
2 cups crushed corn flakes
¼ cup (½ stick) margarine, melted

- In large mixing bowl, combine hash browns, onion, ½ cup (1 stick) margarine, sour cream, soup and cheese and mix well.
- Pour into greased 9 x 13-inch baking dish.
- Combine corn flakes and remaining ¼ cup (½ stick) melted margarine. Sprinkle over top of the casserole.
- Bake uncovered at 350° for 45 to 50 minutes or until bubbly around edges.

This is a "winner" for the best potato casserole you will ever make! It is a particular favorite of the men!

Bacon-Potato Casserole

4 pounds red, new potatoes, unpeeled
1 pound sliced bacon, cooked, drained, crumbled, divided
1 (12 ounce) package shredded Velveeta cheese
1 (8 ounce) package shredded monterey jack cheese, divided
2 onions, chopped
1 (4 ounce) jar chopped pimentos, drained
1 cup mayonnaise
1 (8 ounce) carton sour cream
1 tablespoon dried parsley flakes
1 teaspoon basil
1 ½ teaspoons seasoned salt
1 teaspoon white pepper

- Cut potatoes in half and cook in boiling water with a little salt. Drain well.
- In very large bowl, combine potatoes, half the crumbled bacon, Velveeta cheese, half the jack cheese and all remaining ingredients and mix well.
- Spoon into greased 11 x 14-inch baking dish or two smaller ones. You may cook one and freeze the other.
- Bake uncovered at 325° for 40 minutes or until edges are bubbly.
- Remove from oven and sprinkle remaining jack cheese over top of casserole. Return to oven for about 5 minutes, just until cheese melts.
- Before serving, sprinkle remaining crumbled bacon over top of casserole.

*Did you know that one out of every three meals
in America contains a potato?*

Mashed Potatoes Supreme

1 (8 ounce) package cream cheese, softened
½ cup sour cream
2 tablespoons (¼ stick) margarine, softened
1 envelope ranch salad dressing
8-9 cups instant mashed potatoes, warmed

- With mixer, combine cream cheese, sour cream, margarine and salad dressing and mix well. Add potatoes and stir well.
- Transfer to 1-quart casserole dish.
- Bake at 350° for 25 minutes or until heated thoroughly.

The Irish knew a good thing when they utilized the wonderful "potato". In a world where the French fry reigns, the succulent potato is one of the most versatile of all vegetables.

Sweet Potato Casserole

1 (29 ounce) can sweet potatoes, drained
⅓ cup evaporated milk
¾ cup sugar
¼ cup packed brown sugar
2 eggs, beaten
¼ cup (½ stick) margarine, melted
1 teaspoon vanilla

Topping
1 cup packed light brown sugar
¼ cup (½ stick) margarine, melted
½ cup flour
1 cup chopped pecans

- Place sweet potatoes in mixing bowl and mash slightly with fork.
- Add evaporated milk, sugar, eggs, margarine and vanilla and mix well.
- Pour into greased 7 x 11-inch baking dish or a 2-quart baking dish.
- For topping, combine brown sugar, margarine and flour and mix well.
- Stir in chopped pecans and sprinkle topping over casserole.
- Bake uncovered at 350° for 35 minutes or until crusty on top.

This is a beautiful Thanksgiving dish and perfect for Christmas dinner too. Even people who are "luke warm" about sweet potatoes like this casserole.

Sweet Potato Souffle

2 (15 ounce) cans sweet potatoes, drained, mashed
2 cups sugar
4 eggs, beaten
1 cup half-and-half cream
¼ cup (½ stick) butter, melted
½ teaspoon salt
2 teaspoons vanilla

Topping
1 ½ cups crushed corn flakes
1 cup packed brown sugar
⅛ cup (¼ stick) butter, melted
1 cup chopped pecans
⅓ cup flaked coconut

- In large bowl, combine sweet potatoes, sugar, eggs, cream, butter, salt and vanilla and mix well. (Mixture will be thin.)
- Pour into buttered 2-quart baking dish.
- For topping, combine all ingredients and mix well.
- Sprinkle topping mixture over top of casserole, cover and bake at 350° for 45 minutes.
- Uncover and bake another 15 minutes or until center is firm and the topping is slightly browned.

Happy holiday smiles get bigger when this dish is served.

Speedy Sweet Potatoes

2 (15 ounce) cans sweet potatoes, drained
Pinch salt
1 (8 ounce) can crushed pineapple, undrained
½ cup chopped pecans
2 cups packed brown sugar
½ cup miniature marshmallows, divided
Slight sprinkle of cinnamon and nutmeg

- In 2-quart microwave-safe dish, layer sweet potatoes, pinch of salt, pineapple, pecans, brown sugar and ¼ cup marshmallows.
- Cover loosely and microwave on high for 5 to 6 minutes or until bubby around edges.
- Top with remaining marshmallows. Heat uncovered on high for 30 seconds or until marshmallows puff.
- Sprinkle just a little cinnamon and nutmeg over top of casserole.

Chicken Casseroles

Chicken Dish, WOW!

1 (10 ounce) can cream of chicken soup, undiluted
1 (10 ounce) can fiesta nacho cheese, undiluted
1 (5 ounce) can evaporated milk
2 (15 ounce) cans French-style green beans, drained
1 teaspoon chicken bouillon
4 cups cooked, cubed chicken breast
1 sweet red bell pepper, chopped
2 ribs celery, sliced
¼ cup chopped onion
1 cup chow mein noodles
½ cup slivered almonds
½ teaspoon salt
½ teaspoon white pepper
1 (2.8 ounce) can fried onion rings

- In large bowl, combine soup, fiesta nacho cheese and evaporated milk and mix well.
- Fold in green beans, chicken bouillon, chicken, bell pepper, celery, onion, noodles, almonds, salt and white pepper.
- Spoon into buttered 9 x 13-inch baking dish,
- Bake covered at 350° for 35 minutes. Remove from oven and sprinkle onion rings over casserole.
- Place back in oven and bake another 10 minutes.

This casserole may easily be made ahead of time and baked the next day, just wait to add the onion rings until you put it in the oven.

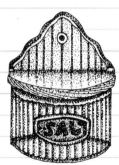

Delightful Chicken Souffle

16 slices white bread, crusts removed
5 boneless, skinless, chicken breast halves, cooked,
thinly sliced diagonally
½ cup mayonnaise
1 cup grated cheddar cheese, divided
5 large eggs
2 cups milk
1 teaspoon seasoned salt
½ teaspoon white pepper
1 (10 ounce) can cream of mushroom soup, undiluted

- Butter 9 x 13-inch baking dish. Line bottom with 8 slices of bread, buttered on 1 side. Cover with sliced chicken. (You could use deli-sliced chicken instead of cooking chicken breasts.)
- Spread chicken slices with mayonnaise and sprinkle with ½ cup cheese. Top with remaining 8 slices bread.
- Beat together eggs, milk, salt and pepper and pour over entire casserole. Refrigerate all day or over night.
- When ready to bake, spread mushroom soup with back of large spoon over top of casserole.
- Bake covered at 350° for 45 minutes.
- Uncover, sprinkle with remaining ½ cup cheddar cheese and return to oven and bake for another 15 minutes.

This is such a fabulous dish for a luncheon. It is really easy to make and you may make it the day before the luncheon. Serve with an English pea salad and slice of cantaloupe or honey dew melon. You don't even need bread with this casserole.

Chicken and Tortilla Dumplings

6 large boneless, skinless chicken breasts
10 cups water
2 celery ribs, chopped
1 onion, chopped
2 tablespoons chicken bouillon
1 (10 ounce) can cream of chicken soup, undiluted
10-11 (8 inch) flour tortillas

- In very large kettle or roaster, place chicken breasts, water, celery and onion. Bring to a boil, then reduce heat and cook for about 30 minutes or until chicken is tender. Remove chicken and set aside to cool.
- Reserve broth in roaster. (You should have about 9 cups of broth.)
- Add chicken bouillon and taste to make sure it is rich and tasty. Add more bouillon if needed and more water if you don't have 9 cups of broth.
- When chicken is cool enough, cut into bite-size pieces and set aside.
- Add chicken soup to broth and bring to a boil.
- Cut tortillas into 2 x 1-inch strips. Add strips, one at a time, to briskly boiling broth mixture and stir constantly.
- When all strips have been added, spoon in chicken, reduce heat to low and simmer 5 to 10 minutes, stirring well but gently, to prevent dumplings from sticking. Your kettle of chicken and dumplings will be very thick. Pour into very large serving bowl and serve hot.

This is not exactly a casserole, but it is a one-dish dinner and these dumplings are wonderful. This recipe is actually easy, it just takes a little time to add tortilla strips, one at a time. Using tortillas are certainly a lot easier than making up biscuit dough for the dumplings!

One-Dish Chicken Bake

¼ cup (½ stick) margarine
1 sweet red bell pepper, chopped
1 onion, chopped
2 ribs celery, chopped
1 (8 ounce) carton sour cream
1 ½ cups half-and-half cream
1 (7 ounce) can chopped green chilies, drained
1 teaspoon chicken bouillon
1 teaspoon seasoned salt
½ teaspoon celery salt
½ teaspoon white pepper
3-4 cups cooked, cubed chicken
1 (16 ounce) package shredded cheddar cheese, divided
1 (2 pound) package frozen hash brown potatoes, thawed

- In saucepan, melt margarine and saute bell pepper, onion and celery.
- In large bowl, combine sour cream, half-and-half, green chilies and seasonings.
- Stir in bell pepper mixture, chicken and half the cheese.
- Fold in the hash brown potatoes. Spoon into greased 9 x 13-inch baking dish.
- Bake, uncovered at 350° for 45 minutes or until casserole is bubbly.
- Remove from oven and sprinkle remaining cheese over top of casserole. Return to oven for about 5 minutes.

This is such a good, basic "meat and potato" dish that the family will love. And for a change of pace, heat some hot, thick and chunky salsa to spoon over the top of each serving.

Three Cheers for Chicken

8 boneless, skinless chicken breast halves
Seasoned salt
Black pepper
6 tablespoons (¾ stick) margarine
1 cup chopped celery
1 onion, chopped
1 small bell pepper, chopped
1 (4 ounce) jar chopped pimentos, drained
1 cup uncooked rice
1 (10 ounce) can cream of chicken soup, undiluted
1 (10 ounce) can cream of celery soup, undiluted
2 cans milk
1 (8 ounce) can sliced water chestnuts, drained
1 ½ cups shredded cheddar cheese

Chicken

- Place chicken breasts in large, greased 11 x 14-inch baking dish and sprinkle with seasoned salt and pepper.
- Melt margarine in large skillet and saute celery, onion and bell pepper. Add pimentos, rice, soups, milk and water chestnuts and mix well.
- Pour mixture over chicken breasts.
- Cook chicken covered at 325° for 60 minutes.
- Uncover and cook another 10 minutes.
- Remove from oven and sprinkle cheese over top of casserole and bake 5 minutes longer.

This chicken casserole is a meal in itself. Just add a tossed green salad and you have a completely, delicious, satisfying meal.

Mr. Mozz's Spaghetti

1 bunch fresh green onions and tops, chopped
1 cup chopped celery
1 sweet red bell pepper, chopped
1 yellow or orange bell pepper, chopped
¼ cup (½ stick) margarine
2 teaspoons seasoned salt
1 teaspoon white pepper
1 tablespoon dried cilantro leaves
1 teaspoon Italian seasoning
1 (7 ounce) package thin spaghetti, cooked, drained
4 cups chopped, cooked chicken or turkey
1 (8 ounce) carton sour cream
1 (16 ounce) jar creamy alfredo sauce
1 (10 ounce) box frozen green peas, thawed
1 (8 ounce) package shredded mozzarella cheese, divided

- In large skillet, saute onions, celery and bell peppers in margarine.
- In large bowl combine onion-pepper mixture, seasonings, spaghetti, chicken, sour cream and alfredo sauce and mix well.
- Fold in peas and half the mozzarella cheese.
- Spoon into greased 10 x 14-inch deep casserole dish and bake covered at 350° for 45 minutes.
- Remove from oven and sprinkle remaining cheese over casserole. Return to oven for about 5 minutes.

(With spaghetti dishes like this, I like to break up the spaghetti before cooking it. It just make it a little easier to serve and to eat.)

This recipe is a little different twist on the always popular chicken spaghetti and if you want to make it even more different twist, just use chopped, cooked ham instead of chicken. This is a wonderful casserole to serve to family or for company. It has great flavor and taste with chicken, pasta and colorful vegetables all in one dish. It's a winner, I promise!

Chicken-Cheese Enchiladas

½ cup water, divided
1 (1.25 ounce) package taco seasoning
2 tablespoons oil, divided
4-5 large boneless, skinless chicken breast halves
1 (16 ounce) jar chunky salsa, divided
1 (12 ounce) package shredded monterey jack cheese,
divided
1 (15 ounce) carton ricotta cheese
1 (4 ounce) can chopped green chilies
1 egg
1 teaspoon dried cilantro
½ teaspoon salt
1 (10.5 ounce) package flour tortillas
Sour cream

- In shallow bowl, combine ¼ cup water, taco seasoning and 1 tablespoon oil and mix well. Place seasoning mixture in baggie.
- Cut chicken breasts into bite-size pieces and place in baggie with seasoning mix. Seal and refrigerate for 1 to12 hours.
- Cook chicken in remaining oil over medium high heat for about 15 minutes.
- Combine ½ cup salsa and remaining ¼ cup water and spoon into greased 9 x 13-inch baking dish. Spread evenly over bottom of dish.
- Stir together 2 ½ cups monterey jack cheese, ricotta cheese, green chilies, egg, cilantro and salt.
- Spoon ⅓ cup cheese mixture down center of each tortilla, top with chicken and roll up.
- Place tortillas, seam-side down, over salsa mixture in dish.
- Drizzle remaining salsa over enchiladas and sprinkle with remaining ½ cup monterey jack cheese.
- Bake uncovered at 350° for 25 minutes. To serve, top with a dab of sour cream.

Chicken

Cheese, Cheese, Cheesy Chicken

1 onion, chopped
½ green bell pepper, chopped
1 sweet red bell pepper, chopped
5 tablespoons (⅔ stick) margarine
1 (10 ounce) can cream of chicken soup, undiluted
1 (4 ounce) can sliced mushrooms
½ teaspoon dried cilantro
½ teaspoon dried basil
1 teaspoon celery salt
½ teaspoon garlic pepper
1 (8 ounce) package egg noodles, cooked al dente, drained
4-5 boneless, skinless chicken breast halves, cooked, cubed
1 (15 ounce) carton ricotta cheese
1 (16 ounce) package shredded cheddar cheese
⅓ cup grated parmesan cheese
1 cup breadcrumbs
3 tablespoons margarine, melted

- In skillet, saute onion and bell peppers in margarine. Remove from heat and stir in soup, mushrooms, cilantro, basil, salt and garlic pepper.
- In large bowl combine noodles, chicken, cheeses and soup-mushroom mixture. Mix well.
- Spoon into buttered 9 x 13-inch baking dish.
- Combine breadcrumbs and margarine and sprinkle over casserole.
- Bake covered at 350° for 45 minutes.

Cheese lovers dig in! It's a winner!

Chicken and Sausage Extraordinaire

1 (6 ounce) box long grain, wild rice
1 pound pork sausage
1 cup chopped celery
2 onions, chopped
1 (4 ounce) jar sliced mushrooms, drained
6 boneless, skinless, chicken breast halves, cooked, sliced
3 tablespoons margarine
¼ cup flour
1 cup whipping cream
1 (14 ounce) can chicken broth
1 teaspoon poultry seasoning
½ teaspoon seasoned salt
½ teaspoon white pepper
⅛ cup (¼ stick) margarine, melted
2 cups crushed crackers

- Cook rice according to package directions and set aside.
- In skillet, brown sausage and remove with a slotted spoon. Saute celery and onions in sausage fat until onion is transparent, not brown. Drain.
- Stir in mushrooms and chicken and set aside.
- Melt margarine in large saucepan, add flour and mix well.
- Over medium heat, slowly add cream, broth and poultry seasoning. Cook, stirring constantly, until mixture is fairly thick. Pour into large bowl.
- Add salt, white pepper, rice, sausage-onion mixture and chicken-mushroom mixture.

(Continued on next page.)

- Spoon into 10 x 14-inch buttered casserole dish.
- Mix together melted margarine and crushed crackers and sprinkle over casserole.
- Bake uncovered at 350° for 40 minutes or until bubbly around edges.

This dish makes enough for about 12 to 14 people so it could easily be placed into 2 smaller baking dishes and one may be frozen. If frozen, thaw in refrigerator and make sure it is thawed in the middle before cooking. Add 5 minutes to cooking time because casserole will be cold.

Jalapeño Chicken

1 onion, chopped
1 bunch fresh green onions, chopped
2 tablespoons margarine
1 (10 ounce) package frozen spinach, thawed, drained
6 jalapenos, seeded, chopped
1 (8 ounce) carton sour cream
2 (10 ounce) cans cream of chicken soup, undiluted
½ teaspoon salt
1 teaspoon ground cumin
1 (12 ounce) package nacho cheese-flavored
tortilla chips, slightly crushed
4-5 cups cooked, chopped chicken
1 (8 ounce) package shredded Mexican 4-cheese blend

- In skillet saute onions in margarine.
- Drain spinach by using several paper towels to squeeze all
  water out of spinach. Add spinach, jalapenos, sour cream,
  chicken soup, salt and ground cumin to onions and mix well.
- In greased 9 x 13-inch baking dish, layer half tortilla chips, half
  chicken, half spinach-soup mixture and cheese. Repeat layers
  without placing last layer of cheese.
- Bake covered at 350° for 40 minutes.
- Uncover and sprinkle remaining cheese over top and return to
  oven for 4 minutes or just until the cheese melts.

*If you like, you may substitute jalapenos for 1 (7 ounce) can chopped
green chilies. It will not be as hot. You may also substitute left-over
turkey for chicken. And, even if you are not a spinach lover, you
will like this chicken-spinach combination.*

Divine Chicken Casserole

1 (16 ounce) package frozen broccoli spears, thawed
1 (10 ounce) box frozen broccoli spears, thawed
1 teaspoon seasoned salt
3 cups diced, cooked chicken
1 (10 ounce) can cream of chicken soup, undiluted
2 tablespoons milk
½ cup mayonnaise
2 teaspoons lemon juice
½ teaspoon white pepper
1 cup shredded cheddar cheese
1 ½ cups round buttery cracker crumbs
3 tablespoons margarine, melted

- Cook broccoli according to package directions and drain. Cut some stems away and discard.
- Place broccoli spears in buttered 9 x 13-inch baking dish and sprinkle seasoned salt over broccoli. Cover with diced chicken.
- In saucepan, combine soup, milk, mayonnaise, lemon juice, white pepper and cheese and heat just enough to be able to pour mixture over broccoli and chicken.
- Combine cracker crumbs and margarine and sprinkle over casserole.
- Bake uncovered at 350° for 35 to 40 minutes or until hot and bubbly.

Chicken Supreme

1 onion, chopped
1 cup sliced celery
3 tablespoons margarine
4 cups diced, cooked chicken breasts
1 (6 ounce) package long grain, wild rice, cooked, reserve
seasoning packet
1 (10 ounce) can cream of celery soup
1 (10 ounce) can cream of chicken soup
1 (4 ounce) jar pimentos
2 (15 ounce) cans French-style green beans, drained
1 cup slivered almonds
1 cup mayonnaise
½ teaspoon salt
1 teaspoon white pepper
2 ½ cups lightly crushed potato chips

- Saute onion and celery in margarine.
- In very large saucepan, combine onion-celery mixture, diced chicken, cooked rice, both soups, pimentos, green beans, almonds, mayonnaise, salt and pepper and mix well.
- Spoon into greased 10 x 14-inch deep baking dish. Sprinkle crushed potato chips over top of casserole.
- Bake uncovered at 350° for 40 minutes or until potato chips are slightly browned.

This recipe is a great way to serve a lot of people (at least 14 to 15 servings). It is really delicious and "sooo" easy. It is a "meal in itself"! It may also be made with green peas instead of green beans. If you want to make in advance and freeze or just refrigerate for the next day, just wait until you are ready to cook the casserole before adding potato chips.

Mexican Chicken

2 cups crushed tortilla chips
4 boneless, skinless chicken breast halves, cooked
1 (15 ounce) can garbanzo beans, drained
1 (15 ounce) can pinto beans, drained
1 (15 ounce) can whole kernel corn, drained
1 (16 ounce) jar hot salsa
1 chopped red onion
2 teaspoons cumin
1 teaspoon dried cilantro leaves
1 green bell pepper, diced
2 teaspoons minced garlic
1 teaspoon salt
1 (8 ounce) package shredded monterey jack cheese
1 (8 ounce) package shredded sharp cheddar cheese
Tomato slices
Sour cream
Fresh green onions

- Grease 9 x 13-inch baking dish and scatter crushed tortilla chips evenly over bottom of dish.
- Cut chicken breasts in thin slices. In large bowl, combine chicken, both beans, corn, salsa, onion, cumin, cilantro leaves, bell pepper, garlic and salt and mix well.
- Spoon half of mixture evenly over chips.
- Combine cheeses, then sprinkle half over mixture. Cover with remaining half of chicken-bean mixture and remaining cheese.
- Bake uncovered at 350° for 35 minutes. Let stand 10 minutes before serving. Garnish with tomato slices, sour cream and chopped fresh onions.

The Chicken Takes the Artichoke

6 boneless, skinned chicken breasts halves
5 tablespoons margarine, divided
1 (14 ounce) jar water-packed artichoke hearts, drained
1 (8 ounce) can sliced water chestnuts, drained
¼ cup flour
½ teaspoon white pepper
⅛ teaspoon ground nutmeg
1 teaspoon summer savory
1 teaspoon dried thyme
1 (14 ounce) can chicken broth
½ cup whipping cream
1 cup grated Swiss cheese
1 cup seasoned breadcrumbs
2 tablespoons margarine, melted

- In skillet, brown chicken breasts in 2 tablespoons margarine. Place chicken breasts in greased 9 x 13-inch baking dish.
- Cut each artichoke heart in half and place artichokes and water chestnuts around chicken.
- In saucepan, melt remaining 3 tablespoons margarine and stir in flour, pepper, nutmeg, summer savory and thyme until smooth and mix well.
- On medium high heat, gradually stir in broth and cook, stirring constantly until broth thickens. Remove from heat and stir in cream and Swiss cheese.
- Blend until cheese melts and pour over chicken, artichokes and water chestnuts.
- Combine breadcrumbs and 2 tablespoons melted margarine and sprinkle over top of casserole.
- Bake uncovered at 350° for 35 minutes.

Creamy Chicken Bake

1 (8 ounce) package egg noodles
1 (16 ounce) package frozen broccoli florets, thawed
¼ cup (½ stick) margarine, melted
1 (8 ounce) package shredded cheddar cheese
1 (10 ounce) can cream of chicken soup, undiluted
1 cup half-and-half cream
¼ teaspoon ground mustard
1 teaspoon seasoned salt
1 teaspoon white pepper
3 cups cooked, cubed chicken breasts
⅔ cup slivered almonds, toasted

- Cook noodles according to package directions and drain; keep warm.
- Cut some stems off broccoli and discard. In large bowl, combine noodles and broccoli.
- Add margarine and cheese and stir until cheese melts.
- Stir in chicken soup, cream, mustard, salt, pepper and chicken. Spoon into buttered 2 ½-quart baking dish.
- Bake covered at 325° for about 25 minutes.
- Remove from oven and sprinkle with slivered almonds and cook for 15 minutes longer.

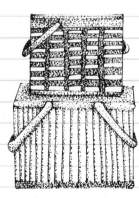

Chicken-Noodle Delight

2 ribs celery, chopped
½ onion, chopped
½ green bell pepper, chopped
½ sweet red bell pepper, chopped
4 tablespoons (⅓ stick) margarine
3 cups cooked, cubed chicken breast
1 (4 ounce) can sliced mushrooms, drained
1 (16 ounce) jar sun-dried tomato alfredo sauce
½ cup half-and-half cream
1 teaspoon salt, optional
1 ½ teaspoons chicken bouillon
1 (8 ounce) package medium egg noodles, cooked, drained

Topping:
1 cup cornflake crumbs
½ cup shredded cheddar cheese
2 tablespoons margarine, melted

- In skillet or large saucepan, combine celery, onion, both bell peppers and margarine and saute for about 5 minutes.
- Remove from heat and add chicken, mushrooms, alfredo sauce, cream, salt, chicken bouillon and noodles and mix well.
- Pour into buttered 3-quart baking dish.
- Combine topping ingredients and sprinkle over casserole.
- Bake uncovered at 325° for 20 minutes or until casserole is bubbly around edges.

This recipe is a hearty main dish and the bell peppers make it a colorful dish as well. It's a great family supper.

Jolly Ole Chicken

1 (6 ounce) package long grain, wild rice with seasonings
1 (16 ounce) can whole berry cranberry sauce
⅓ cup orange juice
3 tablespoons margarine, melted
½ teaspoon curry powder
6 boneless, skinless chicken breast halves
⅔ cup slivered almonds

- Cook rice according to package directions and spoon into greased 9 x 13-inch baking dish.
- In saucepan, combine cranberry sauce, orange juice, margarine and curry powder and heat just enough to mix ingredients well.
- Place chicken breasts over rice and pour cranberry-orange juice mixture over chicken.
- Bake covered at 325° for about 35 minutes.
- Uncover and sprinkle almonds over casserole and return to oven for about 10 to 15 minutes, just until chicken is lightly browned.

This is a little bit of a switch from turkey at Christmas,
and with this casserole you have the chicken
and cranberry sauce all in one dish.

Lemon-Almond Chicken

2 (14.5 ounce) cans cut asparagus, well drained
4 boneless, skinless chicken breast halves,
cut into ½ inch strips
½ teaspoon seasoned salt
3 tablespoons margarine
1 (10 ounce) can cream of asparagus soup
⅔ cup mayonnaise
¼ cup milk
1 sweet red bell pepper, julienned
2 tablespoons lemon juice
1 teaspoon curry powder
¼ teaspoon ground ginger
¼ teaspoon black pepper
½ cup sliced almonds, toasted

- Place asparagus in buttered 7 x 11-inch baking dish and set aside.
- Sprinkle chicken with seasoned salt.
- In large skillet, saute chicken in margarine for about 15 minutes. Spoon chicken strips over asparagus.
- In skillet, combine asparagus soup, mayonnaise, milk, sweet red bell pepper, lemon juice, curry powder, ginger and pepper and heat just enough to mix well.
- Spoon over chicken and sprinkle almonds over top of casserole.
- Bake uncovered at 350° for 35 minutes.

Asparagus, lemon juice, curry powder and almonds give a flavorful punch to an otherwise ordinary chicken dish.

Supper-Ready Chicken

6 boneless, skinless chicken breast halves
2 tablespoons oil
1 cup chopped celery
2 cups sliced zucchini, ½-inch thick
1 (16 ounce) package baby carrots
½ onion, chopped
¼ cup (½ stick) margarine
1 (10 ounce) can cream of chicken soup, undiluted
1 (10 ounce) can fiesta nacho cheese soup, undiluted
1 cup milk or half-and-half cream
½ teaspoon prepared mustard
½ teaspoon dillweed
1 teaspoon dried basil
½ teaspoon pepper

Topping: 2 tablespoons margarine, melted
1 ½ cups soft breadcrumbs or cracker crumbs
½ cup chopped walnuts

- In skillet, brown chicken in oil. Place chicken breasts in greased 9 x 13-inch baking dish and set aside.
- In saucepan, cook celery, zucchini, carrots and onion for about 10 minutes in margarine and very little water and drain.
- In saucepan, combine soups, milk, mustard, dill weed, basil and pepper and heat just enough to mix well.
- Spoon about ¾ cup soup mixture over chicken.
- Combine remaining soup mixture and drained vegetables. Spoon over chicken and soup mixture.
- For topping, combine all ingredients and sprinkle over casserole.
- Bake uncovered at 375° for 35 to 40 minutes or until topping is lightly browned.

You will have one skillet and one saucepan to wash and within 20 minutes you will have creamy chicken plus vegetables ready to go in the oven. And the kids will love the crunchy topping.

Spiced Spanish Chicken

2 cups instant rice, uncooked
4 boneless, skinless, cooked chicken breast halves, cut into strips
1 (15 ounce) can Mexican-style stewed tomatoes, undrained
1 (8 ounce) can tomato sauce
1 (15 ounce) can whole kernel corn, drained
1 (4 ounce) jar diced pimentos, drained
1 teaspoon chili powder
1 teaspoon ground cumin
½ teaspoon salt
¼-½ teaspoon cayenne pepper

- Grease 3-quart baking dish and spread rice evenly over dish. Place chicken strips over top of rice.
- In large bowl, combine stewed tomatoes, tomato sauce, corn, pimentos, chili powder, cumin, salt and cayenne pepper and mix well.
- Slowly and easily pour this mixture over chicken and rice.
- Bake covered at 350° for 1 hour.

The first time you try this, you might want to use only ¼ teaspoon cayenne pepper, unless you know for sure you are prepared for "hot".

Chicken Tetrazzini

½ cup (1 stick) margarine
6 tablespoons flour
1 teaspoon seasoned salt
½ teaspoon pepper
2 (14 ounce) cans chicken broth
1 (8 ounce) carton whipping cream
1 (16 ounce) package linguine, cooked, drained
5-6 boneless, skinless chicken breast halves, cooked, cubed
1 cup sliced fresh mushrooms
2 ribs celery, chopped
1 green bell pepper, chopped
1 (4 ounce) jar diced pimentos, drained
¼ cup chopped fresh parsley
4-5 drops Tabasco
½ cup grated parmesan cheese

- In saucepan over medium heat, melt margarine, add flour, salt and pepper and stir until smooth. Gradually add broth and bring to a boil. Cook and stir constantly until it thickens.
- Remove from heat and stir in cream. If sauce seems too thick, add a little milk.
- Mix 2 cups sauce with linguine, pour into buttered 9 x 13-inch baking dish and spread over casserole dish.
- To remaining sauce, add chicken, mushrooms, celery, bell pepper, pimentos, parsley and Tabasco and mix well. Pour over linguine and sprinkle with parmesan cheese.
- Cover and bake at 350° for about 45 minutes.
- Uncover and bake another 10 minutes.

You may use left-over turkey instead of chicken as long as the turkey is not smoked turkey. The white meat of the turkey is of course better to use than the dark meat.

Three-Cheese Chicken Casserole

1 (8 ounce) package small egg noodles
3 tablespoons margarine
1 green bell pepper, chopped
1 sweet red bell pepper, chopped
½ cup chopped celery
½ cup chopped onion
1 (10 ounce) can cream of chicken soup, undiluted
½ cup milk
1 (6 ounce) jar sliced mushrooms, drained
½ teaspoon black pepper
1 (12 ounce) carton small-curd cottage cheese, drained
4 cups, cooked, diced chicken breasts or turkey breasts
1 (12 ounce) package shredded cheddar cheese
¾ cup freshly grated parmesan

- Cook noodles according to package directions and drain.
- Melt margarine in skillet and saute peppers, celery and onion.
- In large bowl, combine noodles, sauteed mixture, chicken soup, milk, mushrooms, black pepper, cottage cheese, chicken and cheddar cheese. Pour into sprayed 9 x 13-inch baking dish.
- Bake covered at 325° for 35 to 40 minutes or until bubbly around edges of casserole.
- Remove from oven, sprinkle parmesan cheese over casserole and return to oven for 5 minutes.

South-of-the-Border Chicken

8 boneless, skinless chicken breasts
1 cup grated monterey jack cheese
½ cup shredded cheddar cheese
1 (4 ounce) can chopped green chilies
3 tablespoons dehydrated onions
½ cup (1 stick) margarine
2 teaspoons cumin
1 teaspoon chili powder
Tortilla chips, crushed
Cooked white rice

- Pound chicken breasts flat.
- In bowl, mix both cheeses, chilies and onions. Place 2 tablespoons cheese mixture on each chicken breast and roll up placing seam-side down in greased 9 x 13-inch baking dish.
- In a saucepan, melt margarine, add cumin and chili powder and mix well. Pour over chicken.
- Bake covered at 350° for 45 minutes.
- When chicken has 5 minutes left to cook, remove from oven, uncover and top with crushed chips. Return to oven and bake 5 more minutes. Serve over hot cooked rice.

This is really a delicious chicken dish, but it is spicy so be prepared. You need a tossed green salad garnished with avocado slices to complete this delicious meal.

Walnut Chicken

1 (6 ounce) box long grain, wild rice with herbs and
seasonings
2 cups chopped celery
1 onion, chopped
1 cup coarsely chopped walnuts
2 tablespoons butter
2 cups mayonnaise
1 (8 ounce) carton sour cream
1 tablespoon lemon juice
¾ teaspoon seasoned salt
4 cups cooked, cubed chicken
1 cup crushed potato chips
1 (2.8 ounce) can fried onion rings, crushed

- Cook rice according to package directions.
- In skillet, lightly saute celery, onion and walnuts in butter. Add
  mayonnaise, sour cream, lemon juice, seasoned salt and
  chicken and mix well.
- Fold in cooked rice and transfer to greased 9 x 13-inch
  casserole dish.
- Combine potato chips and crushed onion rings and sprinkle
  over top of casserole.
- Bake uncovered at 325° for 25 minutes.

Chicken

Comfort Chicken Plus

1 (6 ounce) box chicken stuffing mix
1 bunch fresh broccoli, cut into florets
1 cup chopped celery
1 cup chopped red bell pepper
2 tablespoons margarine
1 (8 ounce) can whole kernel corn, drained
2 ½ cups finely chopped chicken or left-over turkey
1 envelope hollandaise sauce mix
1 (2.8 ounce) can french-fried onions

- Prepare chicken stuffing mix according to package directions.
- Place broccoli, celery, bell pepper, margarine and ¼ cup water in microwaveable bowl. Cover with wax paper and microwave on high for 1 ½ minutes.
- Add broccoli-celery mixture, corn and chicken to stuffing and mix well. Spoon into buttered 8 x 12-inch baking dish.
- Prepare hollandaise sauce according to package directions but use 1 ¼ cups water instead of 1 cup water stated.
- Pour hollandaise sauce over casserole and sprinkle top with onions.
- Bake uncovered at 325° for 25 minutes.

Chicken Fiesta

1 (13 ounce) bag tortilla chips
4 cups cooked, chopped chicken breasts
1 onion, chopped
1 green bell pepper, chopped
1 sweet red bell pepper, chopped
1 (12 ounce) package shredded Mexican 4-cheese blend
½ teaspoon salt
1 teaspoon chili powder
½ teaspoon black pepper
½ teaspoon ground cumin
2 (10 ounce) cans cream of chicken soup, undiluted
1 (10 ounce) can diced green chilies and tomatoes

- Pour about ⅔ of tortilla chips into sprayed 9 x 13-inch baking dish and crush slightly with palm of your hand.
- In large bowl, combine chicken, onion, peppers, cheese, seasonings, soup and tomatoes and mix well. Spoon mixture over crushed tortilla chips.
- Crush remaining tortilla chips in baggie and spread over casserole.
- Bake uncovered at 325° for 40 minutes.

This is another dish that left-over turkey may be substituted. You may put this recipe together in a matter of minutes. Basically, it involves chopping onion and bell peppers, opening 3 cans and a bag of chips. After about 40 minutes of cooking time, you have a steaming hot, delicious casserole.

Chicken-Orzo Florentine

4 boneless, skinless chicken breast halves
¾ cup uncooked orzo
1 (8 ounce) package fresh mushrooms, sliced
1 (10 ounce) package frozen spinach, thawed, well drained
1 (10 ounce) can golden mushroom soup
½ cup mayonnaise
1 tablespoon lemon juice
½ teaspoon white pepper
1 (8 ounce) package monterey jack cheese
½ cup seasoned Italian breadcrumbs

- Cook chicken in boiling water for about 15 minutes and reserve broth. Cut chicken in bite-size pieces and set aside.
- Pour broth through strainer and cook orzo in remaining broth.
- In large, sprayed skillet, saute mushrooms until tender. Remove from heat and stir in chicken, orzo, spinach, soup, mayonnaise, lemon juice and pepper.
- Fold in half the cheese and mix well.
- Spoon into greased 9 x 13-inch baking dish and sprinkle with remaining cheese and breadcrumbs.
- Bake uncovered at 350° for 35 minutes.

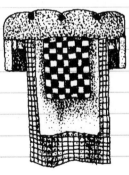

Chicken-Broccoli Deluxe

½ cup (1 stick) margarine
½ cup flour
1 (14 ounce) can chicken broth
1 pint half-and-half cream
1 (16 ounce) package shredded cheddar cheese, divided
1 (3 ounce) package fresh parmesan cheese, grated
2 tablespoons lemon juice
1 tablespoon prepared mustard
½ teaspoon white pepper
2 tablespoons dried parsley
1 tablespoon dried onion flakes
1 teaspoon seasoned salt
½ teaspoon basil
¾ cup mayonnaise
2 (10 ounce) boxes frozen broccoli florets, slightly cooked
5 chicken breast halves, cooked, sliced
1 (7 ounce) box vermicelli
Paprika

- Melt margarine in very large saucepan or roaster. Add flour and mix.
- Over low to medium heat, gradually add chicken broth and cream, stirring constantly, until it thickens, but do not boil.
- Add half cheddar cheese, parmesan cheese, lemon juice, mustard, white pepper, dried parsley, onion flakes, seasoned salt and basil. Heat on low until cheeses melt. Remove from heat and add mayonnaise.
- To cook broccoli, punch small holes in broccoli boxes and microwave 4 minutes. Do not over-cook. Gently add broccoli and chicken slices to sauce.

(Continued on next page.)

- Cook vermicelli according to package directions, drain and pour into greased 10 x 14-inch baking dish.
- Spoon sauce and chicken mixture over vermicelli.
- Bake covered at 325° for 40 minutes.
- Uncover, spread remaining cheese over top and sprinkle a little paprika over cheese. Return to oven for another 5 minutes.

This is another recipe that will serve a lot of hungry people and you may want to divide the ingredients in 2 smaller casseroles. One casserole may be frozen and cooked at a later date. Thaw in refrigerator and make sure it is thawed in the middle before cooking. Add 5 minutes to cooking time.

Chicken-Vegetable Medley

¼ cup (½ stick) margarine
¼ cup flour
1 pint half-and-half cream
½ cup cooking sherry
1 (10 ounce) can cream of chicken soup, undiluted
1 (10 ounce) package frozen broccoli spears, thawed
1 (10 ounce) package frozen cauliflower, thawed
1 sweet red bell pepper, julienned
1 cup chopped celery
1 cup cooked brown rice
4 cups cooked, cubed chicken or turkey
1 (8 ounce) package shredded cheddar cheese
1 cup soft breadcrumbs
3 tablespoons margarine, melted

- In saucepan, melt ¼ (½ stick) margarine, add flour and stir until blended.
- Slowly stir in cream and sherry and cook, stirring constantly, until mixture thickens. Blend in soup until mixture is smooth and set aside.
- Place broccoli, cauliflower, red bell pepper and celery into buttered 9 x 13-inch baking dish.
- Cover with rice, half the sauce and top with chicken. Stir shredded cheese into remaining sauce and pour over chicken.
- Combine breadcrumbs and remaining melted margarine. Sprinkle over casserole.
- Bake uncovered at 350° for about 40 minutes or until casserole is heated thoroughly.

Hurry-Up
Chicken Enchiladas

2 ½-3 cups cooked, shredded chicken breasts
1 (10 ounce) can cream of chicken soup, undiluted
2 cups chunky salsa, divided
8 (6 inch) flour tortillas
1 (10 ounce) can fiesta nacho cheese soup
¼ cup water

- In saucepan, combine chicken (or substitute turkey), soup and ½ cup salsa. Heat on low and stir constantly so mixture will not burn.
- Spread flour tortillas out on your counter and spoon about ⅓ cup chicken mixture down center of each tortilla.
- Roll tortilla around filling and place, seam-side down in buttered 9 x 13-inch baking dish.
- In saucepan, combine nacho cheese, remaining salsa and ¼ cup water and heat just enough to pour mixture. Pour over enchiladas.
- Cover with wax paper and microwave on high, turning several times, for 4-5 minutes or until bubbly.

This is a fast and fun way to make a dish with ingredients at your finger tips and it would be a great dish for the kids to make.

Chicken Martinez

1 (10 ounce) can fiesta nacho cheese soup, undiluted
1 (10 ounce) can cream of chicken soup, undiluted
1 (8 ounce) carton sour cream
1 onion, chopped
1 (10 ounce) can diced tomatoes and green chilies
1 (15 ounce) can black beans, rinsed, drained
1 (15 ounce) can whole kernel Mexicorn, drained
1 teaspoon chili powder
8 flour tortillas, cut into strips
4-5 large boneless, skinless chicken breast halves, cooked, cut into strips
1 (8 ounce) package shredded Mexican 4-cheese blend

- In large bowl, combine both soups, sour cream, onion, tomatoes, black beans, corn and chili powder and mix well.
- Spread small amount of soup-bean mixture over bottom of greased 9 x 13-inch baking dish.
- Arrange half of the tortilla strips over the soup-bean mixture, a layer of chicken, another layer of soup-bean mixture, remaining tortilla strips and remaining chicken. Top with remaining soup-bean mixture.
- Bake covered 350° for 45 minutes or until bubbly.
- Uncover and spread shredded cheese over top of casserole. Return to oven for about 5 minutes, just until the cheese melts.

Sweet Pepper Chicken

6-8 boneless, skinless chicken breasts halves

2 tablespoons oil

⅓ cup cornstarch

⅔ cup sugar

½ cup packed brown sugar

1 teaspoon chicken bouillon granules

1 (15 ounce) can pineapple chunks

1 ½ cups orange juice

½ cup vinegar

¼ cup ketchup

2 tablespoons soy sauce

¼ teaspoon ground ginger

1 sweet red bell pepper, julienned

- In large skillet, brown chicken breasts in oil. Place in buttered 10 x 14-inch baking dish.
- In large saucepan, combine cornstarch, sugar, brown sugar and bouillon granules and mix well.
- Drain pineapple and reserve juice. To the cornstarch mixture in saucepan, add pineapple juice, orange juice, vinegar, ketchup, soy sauce and ginger and mix well.
- On high heat, cook stirring constantly, until mixture thickens. Pour sauce over chicken breasts.
- Bake uncovered at 325° for 45 minutes.
- Remove from oven and add pineapple chunks and julienned bell peppers and bake another 15 minutes.

Garden Chicken

4 boneless, skinless chicken breasts halves, cut into strips
1 teaspoon minced garlic
5 tablespoons butter
1 small yellow squash, julienned
1 small zucchini, julienned
1 sweet red bell pepper, julienned
4 tablespoons flour
1 teaspoon seasoned salt
½ teaspoon salt, optional
½ teaspoon seasoned black pepper
2 teaspoons pesto seasoning
1 (14 ounce) can chicken broth
1 cup half-and-half cream
1 (8 ounce) package angel hair pasta, cooked al dente, drained
⅓ cup shredded parmesan cheese

- In large skillet over medium heat, saute chicken and garlic in butter for about 15 minutes. Remove chicken and set aside.
- With butter in skillet, saute squash, zucchini and sweet bell pepper and cook just until tender-crisp.
- In small saucepan, melt 3 tablespoons butter and add flour, seasoned salt, salt, black pepper and pesto seasoning. Stir to form a smooth paste.
- Over medium high heat, gradually add broth, stirring constantly, until thick. Stir in cream and heat thoroughly.
- In large bowl, combine chicken, vegetables, broth-cream mixture and drained pasta. Transfer to greased 9 x 13-inch casserole dish.

(Contined on next page.)

- Cover and bake at 350° for 30 minutes.
- Uncover and sprinkle parmesan cheese over top of casserole and return to oven for another 5 minutes.

This colorful, delicious casserole is not only flavor packed, but it is also a sight to behold! You can't beat this bountiful dish for family or company.

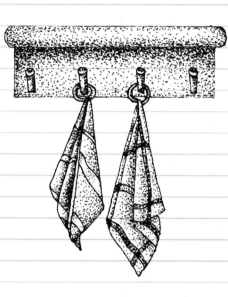

Orange-Spiced Chicken

⅔ cup flour
1 teaspoon salt
½ teaspoon white pepper
½ teaspoon dried basil
¼ teaspoon dried oregano
¼ teaspoon marjoram
¼ teaspoon leaf tarragon
3 tablespoons oil
6 boneless, skinless chicken breast halves
1 (6 ounce) can frozen orange juice concentrate, thawed
½ cup water
½ cup white wine vinegar
⅔ cup packed brown sugar
1 (6 ounce) box long grain, wild rice

- Mix flour, salt, pepper and spices together in a baggie.
- Pour oil into large skillet and heat. Coat chicken in flour mixture, one or two pieces at a time. Brown both sides of chicken breasts in skillet.
- Place browned chicken breasts in greased 9 x 13-inch baking dish.
- In small bowl combine orange juice concentrate, water, vinegar and brown sugar and mix well.
- Spoon about one-half of the orange juice mixture over chicken breasts and bake uncovered at 325° for 30 minutes.
- While chicken is cooking, prepare rice according to package directions and spoon into second 9 x 13-inch baking dish.
- Place cooked chicken breasts over rice and pour remaining orange juice sauce over top of chicken.

Speedy Chicken Pie

1 (12 ounce) package shredded cheddar cheese, divided
1 (10 ounce) package frozen, chopped broccoli, thawed,
drained
2 cups cooked, finely diced chicken breasts
½ cup finely chopped onion
½ cup finely chopped sweet red bell pepper
1 ⅓ cups half-and-half cream
3 eggs
¾ cup biscuit mix
1 teaspoon seasoned salt
¼ teaspoon white pepper

- In bowl, combine 2 cups cheddar cheese, broccoli, chicken, onion and bell pepper. Spread into buttered, 10-inch deep-dish pie plate.
- In mixing bowl, beat together cream, eggs, baking mix, salt and pepper and mix well. Slowly pour cream-egg mixture over broccoli-chicken mixture, but do not stir.
- Bake covered at 375° for 35 minutes or until center of pie is firm.
- Uncover and sprinkle remaining cheese over top. Return to oven for about 5 minutes or just until cheese melts.

Lunch for the girls is not only "speedy", it allows you extra minutes to create a special "out-a-sight" dessert.

Great Crazy Lasagna

1 tablespoon margarine
½ onion, chopped
1 cup fresh mushrooms, sliced
1 (10 ounce) can cream of chicken soup, undiluted
1 (16 ounce) jar alfredo sauce
1 (4 ounce) jar diced pimentos, drained
⅓ cup dry white wine
½ teaspoon dried basil
1 (10 ounce) package frozen chopped spinach, thawed
1 (15 ounce) carton ricotta cheese
⅓ cup grated parmesan cheese
1 egg, beaten
9 lasagna noodles, cooked
3-4 cups cooked chicken, shredded
1 (16 ounce) package shredded cheddar cheese

- In large skillet, melt margarine and saute onion and mushrooms. Stir in soup, alfredo sauce, pimentos, wine and basil. Reserve ⅓ of sauce for top of lasagna.
- Drain spinach well between several layers of paper towels. The spinach needs to be completely drained.
- In bowl, combine spinach, ricotta, parmesan and egg and mix well.
- Spray 10 x 15-inch baking dish with non-stick cooking spray and place 3 noodles in dish. Make sure 10 x 15-inch dish is a full size with a depth of 2 ½ inches.
- Layer with half each of remaining sauce, spinach-ricotta mixture and chicken. The spinach-ricotta mixture will be fairly dry and you will have to spoon it over the sauce and spread out.

(Continued on next page.)

- Sprinkle with 1 ½ cups cheddar cheese. Repeat layering.
- Top with the last 3 noodles and reserved sauce.
- Cover and bake at 350° for 45 minutes.
- Remove from oven and sprinkle remaining cheese on top. Return to oven uncovered and bake another 5 minutes or just until cheese melts. Let casserole stand 10 minutes before serving.

Chicken never got mixed up with any better ingredients!

Chicken and Pasta

4 chicken breast halves, cooked, cubed
2 (8 ounce) cartons sour cream
1 (7 ounce) box ready-cut spaghetti, uncooked
2 (10 ounce) cans cream of chicken soup
1 (4 ounce) can mushrooms, drained
½ cup (1 stick) margarine, melted
¼ teaspoon white pepper
1 cup grated parmesan cheese

- In large bowl, combine chicken, sour cream, spaghetti, chicken soup, mushrooms, margarine and white pepper.
- Pour into greased 9 x 13-inch baking dish.
- Sprinkle cheese on top of casserole.
- Bake covered at 325° for 50 minutes.

How could anything be easier?

Creamed Chicken and Rice

4 cups cooked instant rice
6 tablespoons (¾ stick) margarine, divided
¼ cup flour
2 cups milk
2 teaspoons chicken bouillon granules
½ teaspoon seasoned salt
1 teaspoon parsley flakes
½ celery salt
½ teaspoon white pepper
4 cups cooked, cubed chicken
1 (16 ounce) box processed cheese, cubed
1 (8 ounce) carton sour cream
1 ½ cups round, buttery cracker crumbs

- Spread cooked rice into buttered 9 x 13-inch baking dish and set aside.
- In large saucepan melt 4 tablespoons (½ stick) margarine, stir in flour and mix until smooth. Gradually add milk, bouillon and all seasonings.
- Cook, stirring constantly, on medium heat for about 2 minutes or until sauce thickens.
- Reduce heat and add chicken, cheese and sour cream and stir until cheese melts.
- Spoon over rice in baking dish. Melt remaining 2 tablespoons (¼ stick) margarine and toss with cracker crumbs. Sprinkle over casserole.
- Bake uncovered at 325° for 35 minutes or until heated thoroughly.

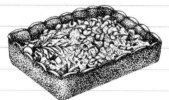

Taco Casserole

2 (10 ounce) cans fiesta nacho cheese soup, undiluted
½ cup milk
1 (15 ounce) can whole kernel corn, drained
1 envelope taco seasoning
1 sweet red bell pepper, chopped
1 onion, chopped
½ teaspoon salt
1 teaspoon ground cumin
1 (12 ounce) package shredded cheddar-jack cheese
1 (13 ounce) package corn tostitos, slightly crushed
3-4 cups cooked, diced chicken breasts or turkey
1 (4 ounce) can sliced black olives

- In large bowl, combine soup, milk, corn, taco seasoning, bell pepper, onion, salt and cumin and mix well.
- In greased 9 x 13-inch baking dish, place a layer of half crushed tostitos, half chicken, half soup mixture and half cheese. Repeat layers ending with cheese on top.
- Bake covered at 325° for 40 minutes or until casserole is bubbly around edges.
- When ready to serve, sprinkle top of casserole with black olives.

Not JUST Chicken

3 cups cooked, cubed chicken or turkey
3 cups fully cooked cubed ham
1 (8 ounce) package shredded cheddar cheese
1 (15 ounce) can English peas, drained
1 onion, chopped
3 ribs celery, chopped
¼ cup (½ stick) margarine
⅓ cup plus 1 tablespoon flour
1 pint half-and-half cream
½ cup milk
1 teaspoon dillweed
⅛ teaspoon ground mustard
⅛ teaspoon ground nutmeg
¾ teaspoon seasoned salt
Hot, cooked instant brown rice
⅓ cup chopped walnuts

- In large bowl combine chicken, ham, cheese and English peas.
- In very large saucepan, saute onion and celery in margarine until tender. Add flour and stir to make a paste.
- Gradually add cream, milk, dillweed, mustard, nutmeg and seasoned salt. Heat, stirring constantly, until mixture thickens.
- Add thickened cream mixture to chicken-ham mixture and mix well.
- Spoon into greased 2 ½-quart baking dish. Use a pretty baking dish that you can place on the table to serve.
- Cover and bake at 350° for 20 minutes.
- Spoon chicken and ham casserole over hot brown rice.

This is a great recipe for left-over ham or turkey. It is really a "quick fix" for the family.

Chicken-Ham Lasagna

1 (4 ounce) can chopped mushrooms, drained
1 large onion, chopped
¼ cup (½ stick) margarine
½ cup flour
1 teaspoon seasoned salt
¼ teaspoon white pepper
⅛ teaspoon ground nutmeg
1 (14 ounce) can chicken broth
1 ¾ cups half-and-half cream
1 (3 ounce) package grated parmesan cheese
1 (16 ounce) package frozen broccoli florets, thawed
9 lasagna noodles, cooked, drained
1 ½ cups cooked, finely diced ham, divided
1 (12 ounce) package shredded monterey jack cheese, divided
2 cups cooked, shredded chicken breasts

- In large skillet, saute mushrooms and onion in margarine. While on medium heat, stir in flour, salt, pepper and nutmeg and stir until well blended.
- Gradually stir in broth and cream, cook and stir for about 2 minutes or until thickened. Stir in parmesan cheese.
- Cut stems off broccoli and discard. Cut broccoli into smaller pieces. Add to cream mixture.
- Spread about ½ cup cream-broccoli mixture in greased 11 x 14-inch baking dish. Layer with three noodles, ⅓ of remaining broccoli mixture, ½ cup ham and 1 cup monterey jack cheese.
- Top with 3 more noodles, ⅓ of the broccoli mixture, 1 cup ham and 1 cup monterey jack cheese.
- Pour remaining cream-broccoli mixture over cheese.
- Bake covered at 350° for 50 minutes or until bubbly.
- Sprinkle with remaining cheese. Let stand for 15 minutes before cutting into squares to serve.

Who says you have to have a tomato sauce for lasagne?

A Chinese Garden

1 (6 ounce) package Rice-A-Roni fried rice with almonds and
oriental seasoning
2 tablespoons margarine
1 onion, chopped
2 cups chopped celery
1 (15 ounce) can Chinese vegetables, drained
1 (8 ounce) can sliced bamboo shoots
3 ½ cups cooked, chopped chicken
1 (10 ounce) can cream of chicken soup
1 cup mayonnaise
2 tablespoons soy sauce
½ teaspoon garlic powder
½ teaspoon pepper
1 cup chop mein noodles

- Cook rice according to package directions and set aside.
- Heat margarine in large skillet and saute onion and celery. Add
  Chinese vegetables, bamboo shoots and chicken and mix well.
- In saucepan, heat chicken soup, mayonnaise, soy sauce, garlic
  powder and pepper just enough to mix well.
- In large bowl, combine rice, vegetable-chicken mixture and
  soup mixture and mix well.
- Transfer to greased 3-quart baking dish.
- Sprinkle chow mein noodles over casserole.
- Bake uncovered at 350° for 35 minutes.

*This would be stretching a point to call this an authentic Chinese
recipe, but this combination of ingredients makes a great tasting
casserole. Try it, you'll like it!*

Chicken, Veggies and Cashews

3 ½ cups cooked, cubed chicken breasts
2 (10 ounce) cans cream of chicken soup, undiluted
2 (15 ounce) cans chop suey vegetables, drained
1 (8 ounce) can sliced water chestnuts, drained
¾ cup chopped cashew nuts
1 green bell pepper, chopped
1 onion, chopped
1 cup celery, chopped
¼ teaspoon Tabasco
¼ teaspoon curry powder
1 ¼ cups chow mein noodles

- In large bowl, combine chicken, soup, vegetables, water chestnuts, cashew nuts, green pepper, onion, celery, Tabasco and curry powder. Stir to mix well.
- Spoon into 9 x 13-inch baking dish sprayed with non-stick vegetable spray. Sprinkle chow mein noodles over top of casserole.
- Bake uncovered at 350° for 35 minutes or until bubbly at edges of casserole. Let set 5 minutes before serving.

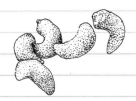

Chicken Quesadillas

2 cups cooked, shredded chicken
¾ cup picante sauce
3 fresh green onions, chopped
½ teaspoon ground cumin
¼ teaspoon salt
4 (8 inch) flour tortillas
Softened margarine
1 cup Mexican 4-cheese blend
Guacamole

- In skillet over medium high heat, combine and cook chicken, picante, onions, cumin and salt for about 5 minutes, just until it is thoroughly hot.
- Brush one side of each tortilla with margarine.
- Place half of chicken-mixture on 1 tortilla, the other half on a second tortilla.
- Sprinkle cheese equally over the two tortillas and place other two tortillas, margarine side down, over cheese.
- Place on lightly greased baking sheet and bake at 400° for about 10 minutes or until crisp. To serve cut into wedges. Serve with guacamole.

Baked Chicken Salad

4 cups cooked, chopped chicken breasts
¾ cup mayonnaise
¼ cup chopped onion
1 ½ cups chopped celery
4 hard-boiled eggs, chopped
1 (4 ounce) can chopped pimentos, drained
⅔ cup slivered almonds, toasted
1 cup shredded cheddar cheese
¾ teaspoon seasoning salt
½ teaspoon white pepper
2 tablespoons lemon juice
1 (10 ounce) can cream of chicken soup
1 ½ cups crushed potato chips

- In large bowl, combine all ingredients except crushed potato chips. Spoon into buttered 9 x 13-inch baking dish.
- Cover and refrigerate for at least 8 hours. Flavor improves when refrigerated overnight before cooking.
- When ready to bake, top casserole with crushed potato chips.
- Bake uncovered at 325° for 35 to 40 minutes or until potato chips are lightly browned.

Turkey and Ham Tetrazzini

1 (7 ounce) box thin spaghetti, cooked, drained
½ cup slivered almonds, toasted
1 (10 ounce) can cream of mushroom soup, undiluted
1 (10 ounce) can cream of chicken soup, undiluted
¾ cup milk
2 tablespoons dry white wine
2 ½ cups diced, cook left-over turkey
2 cups fully cooked, left-over diced ham
½ cup chopped green bell pepper
½ cup chopped sweet red bell pepper
½ cup halved pitted ripe olives
1 (8 ounce) package shredded cheddar cheese

- Rinse cooked spaghetti with cold water to maintain firmness.
- Mix together almonds, both soups, milk and wine in large bowl.
- Stir in spaghetti, turkey, ham, chopped peppers and pitted olives. Spoon into buttered 9 x 13-inch baking dish.
- Bake covered at 350° for 35 minutes or until casserole is hot and bubbly.
- Remove cover and sprinkle top of casserole with cheese. Return to oven for 5 minutes.

This is another old-fashioned dish modified to meet today's need for a "hurry-up meal" while retaining that nostalgic flavor.

Creamy Turkey Enchiladas

2 tablespoons margarine
1 onion, finely chopped
3 green onions and tops, finely chopped
½ teaspoon garlic powder
½ teaspoon seasoned salt
1 (7 ounce) can chopped green chilies
¼ teaspoon cayenne pepper
2 (8 ounce) packages cream cheese, softened
3 cups diced, cooked turkey or chicken
8 (8 inch) flour tortillas
2 (8 ounce) cartons whipping cream
1 (16 ounce) package shredded Mexican 4-cheese blend

- In large skillet, add margarine and saute onions. Add garlic powder, seasoned salt, green chilies and cayenne pepper.
- Stir in cream cheese. Heat and stir just until cream cheese melts. Add diced turkey or chicken.
- Spread out 8 tortillas and spoon about 3 heaping tablespoons of turkey-cream cheese mixture on each tortilla. Use all the turkey mixture.
- Roll up tortillas and place seam-side down in lightly greased large 11 x 15-inch baking dish. Pour whipping cream over enchiladas and sprinkle cheese over enchiladas.
- Bake uncovered at 350° for 30 minutes or just until cream and cheese are bubbly, but not brown.

Forget about the calories. These enchiladas are worth it! Every time I make these I get raves. You need to use a long, wide spatula to serve these enchiladas. (Just in case you happen to have a couple enchiladas left over, heat them in the microwave and spoon hot salsa over them. You'll love these left-overs).

Jazzy Turkey and Dressing

1 (6 ounce) package stuffing mix with seasoning packet
3 cups cooked, diced turkey
1 (15 ounce) can golden hominy, drained
1 (7 ounce) can chopped green chilies, drained
½ cup chopped red bell pepper
2 tablespoons dried parsley flakes
1 (10 ounce) can cream of chicken soup, undiluted
1 (8 ounce) carton sour cream
½ cup water
2 tablespoons (¼ stick) margarine, melted
2 teaspoons ground cumin
½ teaspoon salt
1 cup shredded mozzarella cheese

- In large mixing bowl, combine all ingredients except cheese. Mix well and pour into greased 9 x 13-inch baking dish.
- Bake covered at 350° for 35 minutes.
- Uncover, sprinkle with cheese and return to oven. Bake an additional 5 minutes or just until cheese melts.

Tempting Chicken and Veggies

1 ½ pounds chicken breast tenderloins
3 tablespoons (⅓ stick) margarine
1 (6.2 ounce) box Rice A Roni fried rice and seasoning
packet
2 ½ cups water
⅛ teaspoon cayenne pepper
¼ cup chopped sweet red bell pepper
1 (10 ounce) package frozen broccoli spears, thawed
1 (10 ounce) package frozen corn, thawed

• In skillet, brown chicken tenderloins in margarine. Remove
  chicken to large mixing bowl.
• In same skillet with remaining butter, sauté rice until slightly
  browned and spoon into bowl with chicken.
• Add water, cayenne pepper, bell pepper, broccoli spears and
  corn and mix well.
• Spoon into sprayed 9 x 13-inch baking dish.
• Cover and cook at 325° for 25 minutes or until rice and
  vegetables are tender.

Beef
Casseroles

Beef and Noodles al Grande

1 ½-2 pounds lean ground beef
1 onion, chopped
1 green bell pepper, chopped
1 (16 ounce) box Mexican-style processed cheese, cubed
1 (10 ounce) can fiesta nacho cheese soup
1 (15 ounce) can stewed tomatoes
1 (10 ounce) can tomatoes and green chilies
1 (8 ounce) can whole kernel corn, drained
1 ½ teaspoons salt
½ teaspoon chili powder
¼ teaspoon ground mustard
½ teaspoon seasoned pepper
1 (8 ounce) package medium egg noodles
¼ cup (½ stick) margarine, cut into 4-5 slices
1 cup shredded cheddar cheese

- In skillet, cook beef, onion and bell pepper until beef is no longer pink and vegetables are tender. Drain.
- Remove from heat, add processed cheese and stir until cheese melts.
- In large mixing bowl, combine fiesta nacho cheese, stewed tomatoes, tomatoes and green chilies, corn, salt, chili powder, mustard and pepper. Add beef mixture and mix well.
- Cook egg noodles according to package directions and drain well.
- While noodles are still very hot, add margarine and stir until margarine melts.
- Stir noodles in with tomato-beef mixture. Transfer to greased 10 x 14-inch baking dish.
- Cover and bake at 350° for 45 minutes.
- Uncover and sprinkle cheese over casserole and return to oven for 4 to 10 minutes.

This is an ideal casserole to make ahead of time for a quick and easy supper and it will serve about 14 people. These blended flavors create a delicious dish that people always remember.

Zesty Rice and Beef

1 pound lean ground round steak
1 onion, chopped
1 green bell pepper, chopped
2 ½ cups cooked rice
1 (15 ounce) can whole kernel corn, drained
1 (15 ounce) can Mexican-style stewed tomatoes
1 (15 ounce) can diced tomatoes
2 teaspoons chili powder
1 teaspoon garlic powder
1 teaspoon salt
1 (8 ounce) package cubed Velveeta cheese
1 cup buttery cracker crumbs
½ cup chopped pecans or walnuts
2 tablespoons margarine, melted

- In large skillet or roaster, cook beef, onion and green pepper over medium heat until beef is no longer pink. Drain well.
- Add rice, corn, stewed tomatoes, diced tomatoes, chili powder, garlic powder and salt and bring to a boil. Remove from heat.
- Stir in Velveeta cheese until cheese melts. Spoon into greased 9 x 13-inch baking dish.
- Combine cracker crumbs, pecans and melted margarine. Sprinkle over top of casserole.
- Bake uncovered at 350° for 25 minutes or until casserole is bubbly hot.

Stroganoff Casserole

1 (12 ounce) package medium egg noodles
1 ½ pounds lean ground beef
1 onion, chopped
1 green bell pepper, seeded, chopped
1 cup chopped celery
½ cup beef broth
1 (6 ounce) can tomato paste
1 (4 ounce) can sliced mushrooms, drained
1 teaspoon dried oregano
½ teaspoon garlic powder
½ teaspoon salt
1 (8 ounce) carton sour cream
1 (16 ounce) container small curd cottage cheese
1 (8 ounce) package shredded mozzarella cheese
1 cup shredded cheddar cheese

Beef

- Cook noodles according to package directions, drain and keep warm.
- In large skillet, cook ground beef until it crumbles and is no longer pink. Drain well.
- Stir in onion, bell pepper and celery. Cover and cook over medium-high heat for about 15 minutes, stirring occasionally.
- Stir in beef broth, tomato paste, mushrooms, oregano, garlic powder and salt and set aside.
- In large bowl combine sour cream and cottage cheese and mix well. Stir in cooked noodles and toss to coat.
- Spread half this mixture into buttered 9 x 13-inch baking dish.
- Top with half the meat-vegetable mixture, half the mozzarella cheese and half the cheddar cheese. Repeat layers of remaining noodles and meat-vegetable mixture.
- Cover and bake at 350° for about 25 minutes.
- Remove from oven and sprinkle with remaining cheeses. Bake uncovered for another 5 minutes.

To make slicing mushrooms easy, use an egg slicer! Try it, it works great!

Enchilada Casserole

1 ½ pounds lean ground beef
Salt and pepper
1 package taco seasoning mix
1 ¼ cups water
Oil
8 flour or corn tortillas
1 cup shredded cheddar cheese
1 onion, chopped
1 (10 ounce) can enchilada sauce
1 (7 ounce) can green chilies
1 ½ cups grated monterey jack cheese
1 (8 ounce) carton sour cream

- Brown beef in skillet with salt and pepper until it crumbles and is no longer pink. Drain well.
- Add taco seasoning mix and water to beef and simmer 5 minutes or until most of the liquid is gone.
- In another skillet pour just enough oil to cover bottom of skillet and heat until oil is hot.
- Cook tortillas one at a time, until soft and limp, about 5 to 10 seconds on each side. Drain on paper towels.
- As you are cooking tortillas, spoon ⅓ cup meat mixture into center of each well drained tortilla.
- Sprinkle with small amount of cheddar cheese and 1 spoon full of chopped onion. Roll up and place seam-side down in greased 9 x 13-inch baking dish.
- After filling all tortillas, add enchilada sauce and green chilies to remaining meat mixture. Spoon over tortillas.
- Cover and bake at 350° for about 30 minutes.
- Uncover and sprinkle remaining cheddar cheese and monterey jack cheese over casserole.
- Return to oven just until cheese melts. Place dabs of sour cream over enchiladas to serve.

Enchilada Casserole Grande

1 ½ pounds lean ground beef
½ teaspoon minced garlic
1 (8 ounce) package shredded colby-jack cheese blend
1 onion, chopped
1 (10 ounce) can cream of chicken soup
1 (5 ounce) can evaporated milk
1 (8 ounce) box processed cheese, cubed
1 (.4 ounce) envelope ranch dip mix
1 (7 ounce) can chopped green chilies
1 (2 ounce) jar chopped pimento, drained
Water
12 (8 inch) corn tortillas

- Cook beef and garlic until beef crumbles and is no longer pink. Drain well.
- Stir in shredded colby-jack cheese and onion and set aside.
- In saucepan over medium heat, combine soup, evaporated milk and processed cheese and stir until cheese melts.
- Add dip mix, chilies and pimento.
- Pour water to depth of 1-inch in skillet and heat on high. (Keep heat on medium so water will stay hot.) Dip tortillas, 1 at a time, into hot water using tongs. Soak 2 to 3 seconds, remove and drain.
- Spoon about ⅓ cup meat mixture onto 1 side of each tortilla. Roll up tightly and place seam-side down in greased 9 x 13-inch baking dish.
- Spoon cheese sauce over enchiladas.
- Bake covered at 350° for 30 minutes.
- Uncover and bake another 10 minutes.

Meatball Veggies

1 ½ pounds lean ground beef
2 tablespoons ketchup
1 egg
⅓ cup seasoned breadcrumbs
2 tablespoons dried onion flakes
1 teaspoon seasoned salt
1 (15 ounce) can whole kernel corn, drained
2 (10 ounce) cans diced tomatoes and green chilies
1 onion, chopped
⅔ cup water
2 tablespoons corn starch
½ teaspoon dried thyme
2 teaspoons Italian seasoning
½ teaspoon salt
¼ teaspoon seasoned pepper
1 teaspoon minced garlic
1 (28 ounce) package frozen hash brown potatoes
¼ cup (½ stick) margarine, melted
1 (8 ounce) package shredded cheddar cheese

- In a mixing bowl, combine beef, ketchup, egg, breadcrumbs, onion and salt.
- Shape into 1-inch balls and place on baking dish. Bake at 375° for about 20 minutes or until meatballs are browned.
- In large saucepan, combine corn, tomatoes, green chilies, onion, water, cornstarch, thyme, Italian seasoning, salt, seasoned pepper and garlic and mix well. Cover and simmer for about 10 minutes
- Stir in meatballs and set aside.
- Place hash browns in greased 9 x 13-inch baking dish and slowly drizzle melted margarine over potatoes.
- Spoon meatball-tomato mixture over hash browns.
- Cover and bake at 350° for 45 minutes.
- Remove from oven, sprinkle cheese over top of casserole and return to oven for 10 minutes.

Just Say "Hot"

2 pounds lean ground beef
1 onion, chopped
1 green bell pepper, chopped
1 tablespoon chili powder
1 tablespoon ground cumin
1 teaspoon salt
1 (15 ounce) can ranch-style beans, undrained
1 (15 ounce) can whole kernel corn, drained
6 corn tortillas, cut into strips
1 (8 ounce) package shredded cheddar cheese
1 (10 ounce) can diced tomatoes and green chilies
1 (10 ounce) can fiesta nacho cheese soup
1 ½ cups crushed tortilla chips

- In skillet, brown beef, onion and bell pepper and cook, stirring occasionally, for about 10 minutes. Drain well.
- Stir in chili powder, cumin and salt.
- Spoon meat mixture into greased 9 x 13-inch baking dish.
- Make layers of beans, corn, half the tortilla strips and half the cheese. Continue the layers with remaining tortilla strips and remaining cheese.
- In saucepan, combine tomatoes and chilies with fiesta nacho cheese soup and heat just enough to mix well. Spoon this mixture over top of cheese.
- Cover and bake at 350° for 20 minutes.
- Remove from oven and sprinkle crushed tortilla chips over top of casserole. Return to oven for another 20 minutes.

Chili Relleno Casserole

1 pound lean ground beef
1 bell pepper, chopped
1 onion, chopped
1 (4 ounce) can chopped green chilies
1 teaspoon oregano
1 teaspoon dried cilantro leaves
¾ teaspoon garlic powder
½ teaspoon salt
½ teaspoon black pepper
2 (4 ounce) cans whole green chilies
1 ½ cups grated monterey jack cheese
1 ½ cups grated sharp cheddar cheese
3 large eggs
1 tablespoon flour
1 cup half-and-half cream

- In skillet, brown meat with bell pepper and onion. Add chopped green chilies, oregano, cilantro, garlic powder, salt and pepper.
- Seed whole chilies and spread on bottom of greased 9 x 13-inch baking dish.
- Cover with meat mixture and sprinkle with cheeses.
- Combine eggs and flour and beat with fork until fluffy.
- Add half-and-half cream, mix and pour slowly over top of meat in casserole.
- Bake uncovered at 350° for 35 minutes or until it is lightly browned.

Chinese Beef
with Veggies and Cashews

1 ½ pounds lean ground beef
1 onion, chopped
1 green bell pepper, chopped
2 cups chopped celery
1 cup uncooked rice
¼ cup soy sauce
½ teaspoon Tabasco sauce
½ teaspoon salt
1 (15 ounce) can Chinese vegetables, drained
1 (4 ounce) can sliced mushrooms, drained
1 ¼ cups cashew nuts
1 (10 ounce) can golden mushroom soup
2 cups water
1 ½ teaspoon beef bouillon
1 ½ cups chow mein noodles

- In skillet, brown beef and stir well to break up meat.
- In large bowl, combine onion, bell pepper, celery, rice, soy
  sauce, tabasco, salt, Chinese vegetables, mushrooms and
  cashew nuts.
- In saucepan, combine soup, water and beef bouillon and heat
  just enough to mix well.
- Combine beef and soup mixture with onion-vegetable mixture.
- Pour into greased 9 x 13-inch baking dish. Cover and bake at
  350° for 50 minutes.
- Remove from oven and sprinkle noodles over casserole. Bake
  uncovered another 20 minutes.

*This is good! It takes very little time to prepare and you will love
serving it to your family or friends. A Chinese slaw goes great with
it and it is easy to prepare. Everything can be made ahead of time.*

Cabbage Rolls Along

1 large head cabbage, cored
1 ½ pounds lean ground beef
1 egg, beaten
3 tablespoons ketchup
⅓ cup seasoned breadcrumbs
2 tablespoons dried minced onion flakes
1 teaspoon seasoned salt
2 (15 ounce) cans Italian stewed tomatoes
¼ cup cornstarch
3 tablespoons brown sugar
2 tablespoons wocestershire sauce

- In large kettle, place head of cabbage in boiling water for 10 minutes or until outer leaves are tender. Drain well. Rinse in cold water and remove 10 large outer leaves. (To get that many large leaves, you may have to put 2 smaller leaves together to make one roll.) Set aside.
- Take remaining cabbage and slice or grate in slivers. Place in bottom of greased 9 x 13-inch baking dish.
- In large bowl combine ground beef, egg, ketchup, breadcrumbs, onion flakes and seasoned salt and mix well.
- Place about ½ cup meat mixture packed together on each cabbage leaf.
- Fold in sides and roll up leaf to completely enclose filling. You may have to remove thick vein from cabbage leaves for easier rolling.
- Place each rolled-up leaf over grated cabbage. Place stewed tomatoes in large saucepan.
- Combine cornstarch, brown sugar and worcestershire sauce and spoon mixture into tomatoes. Cook on high heat, stirring constantly, until stewed tomatoes thicken. Pour over cabbage rolls.
- Cover and bake at 325° for 1 hour.

This is a wonderful family recipe and a super way to get the kids to eat cabbage. Everyone who has ever had a garden has probably made some version of these well-loved cabbage rolls.

Beef

Summer Cabbage Deluxe

1 ½ pounds lean ground beef
1 (16 ounce) package frozen broccoli florets, thawed
1 medium head cabbage, cored, coarsely chopped
1 teaspoon salt, optional
½ teaspoon sugar
1 (8 ounce) carton sour cream
½ cup mayonnaise
2 cups shredded white cheddar cheese
1 teaspoon seasoned salt
1 teaspoon white pepper
1 ½ cups soft breadcrumbs
2 tablespoons margarine, melted

- In large skillet, cook beef until meat is fairly brown.
- Lay broccoli florets out on a cutting board and cut off most of the stems.
- Place broccoli florets, cabbage, salt, sugar and about ¾ cup water in large saucepan. Cook over medium heat about 10 minutes, stirring occasionally, only until vegetables are tender-crisp. Drain well.
- In large bowl, combine beef, broccoli-cabbage mixture, sour cream, mayonnaise, white cheddar cheese, seasoned salt and white pepper. Transfer to buttered 3-quart baking dish.
- Combine breadcrumbs and margarine and sprinkle over casserole.
- Bake uncovered at 350° for 25 minutes or until breadcrumbs are slightly browned.

Beef

Taco Pie

1 ½ pounds lean ground beef
½ green bell pepper, chopped
1 teaspoon oil
½ teaspoon salt
1 (15 ounce) can Mexican stewed tomatoes
1 cup water
1 tablespoon chili powder
¼ teaspoon garlic powder
1 ½ cups shredded cheddar cheese
1 (6 ounce) package corn muffin mix
1 egg
⅔ cup milk

- In large skillet, brown ground beef and bell pepper in oil and drain well.
- Add salt, tomatoes, water, chili powder and garlic powder. Cook on medium heat for about 10 minutes or until most of liquid is gone.
- Pour into greased 9 x 13-inch baking dish. Sprinkle cheese on top.
- Combine corn muffin mix, egg and milk and beat well. Pour over top of cheese.
- Bake at 375° for 25 minutes or until corn muffin mix is lightly brown.
- Remove from oven and let set about 10 minutes before serving.

Enchilada Lasagna

1 ½ pounds lean ground beef
1 onion, chopped
1 teaspoon minced garlic
1 (15 ounce) can enchilada sauce
1 (15 ounce) can stewed tomatoes
1 teaspoon cumin
½ teaspoon salt
1 egg
1 (12 ounce) carton small curd cottage cheese
1 (12 ounce) package shredded 4-cheese blend, divided
8 (8 inch) corn tortillas, torn
1 cup shredded cheddar cheese

- In large skillet cook beef, onion and garlic until meat is no longer pink.
- Stir in enchilada sauce, tomatoes, cumin and salt. Bring mixture to a boil, then reduce heat and simmer uncovered for 20 minutes.
- In small bowl, combine egg and cottage cheese.
- Spread one-third of meat sauce in greased 9 x 13-inch baking dish. Top with half of 4-cheese blend, tortillas and cottage cheese mixture. Repeat layers.
- Top with remaining meat sauce and sprinkle remaining 1 cup cheddar cheese.
- Cover and bake at 325° for 25 minutes. Uncover and bake 10 more minutes.

Italian Manicotti

1 pound lean ground beef
2 teaspoons minced garlic
2 onions, chopped
1 (28 ounce) can diced tomatoes, undrained
1 (8 ounce) package fresh mushrooms, sliced
1 teaspoon fennel seed
2 teaspoons basil
1 teaspoon Italian seasoning
½ teaspoon seasoned salt
½ teaspoon pepper
2 (10 ounce) boxes frozen spinach, thawed, well drained
½ cup grated parmesan cheese, divided
1 (16 ounce) carton small curd cottage cheese, drained
¼ teaspoon ground nutmeg
½ teaspoon pepper
14 manicotti shells, cooked al dente

- In large skillet, brown ground beef, then add garlic and onion and reduce heat to low. Simmer for 10 minutes and drain.
- Add tomatoes and liquid, mushrooms, fennel seed, basil, Italian seasoning, seasoned salt and pepper and stir to mix well. Bring to boil, reduce heat and simmer for 10 minutes, stir occasionally.
- In separate bowl, stir together well drained spinach, half the parmesan, cottage cheese, nutmeg and pepper.
- In sprayed 9 x 13-inch baking dish, spoon about one third of beef sauce evenly over bottom of dish.
- Fill manicotti shells with spinach mixture and place on beef layer in baking dish. Repeat until all spinach mixture has been used in manicotti shells.
- Pour remaining beef sauce evenly over manicotti shells to cover. Sprinkle remaining parmesan cheese over top.
- Cover and bake at 325° for 1 hour and 30 minutes or until shells are tender.

Beef

Meatball Casserole

1 ¼ pounds lean ground beef
2 tablespoons ketchup
1 teaspoon Italian seasoning
1 egg
1 teaspoon minced garlic
¼ cup seasoned breadcrumbs
¼ cup grated parmesan cheese
1 ¼ pounds lean ground beef
1 loaf Italian bread, cut into 1-inch slices
1 (8 ounce) package cream cheese, softened
½ cup mayonnaise
1 teaspoon Italian seasoning
½ teaspoon seasoned pepper
1 (8 ounce) package shredded mozzarella cheese, divided
1 (28 ounce) jar spaghetti sauce
½ cup water
1 ½ teaspoons minced garlic
¾ teaspoon salt

- In large mixing bowl, combine beef, ketchup, Italian seasoning, egg, minced garlic, breadcrumbs and parmesan cheese. Shape into small balls and place on rack in shallow baking pan.
- Bake at 375° for 20 minutes or until they are no longer pink.
- While meat is cooking, arrange bread in single layer in ungreased 9 x 13-inch baking pan. (All of the bread might not be needed.)
- In mixing bowl, combine and beat cream cheese, mayonnaise, Italian seasoning and pepper and spread over bread slices. Sprinkle with 1 cup mozzarella.

(Continued on next page.)

- In bowl combine spaghetti sauce, water, garlic and salt. Arrange meatballs over bread-cheese mixture and spoon spaghetti sauce over meatballs.
- Bake uncovered at 350° for 25 minutes.
- Remove from oven and sprinkle remaining cheese over top of casserole. Return to oven for 10 minutes. Let casserole stand for about 10 minutes before serving.

Yes, this is a crazy sounding recipe, but "wow" is it ever good!
It is really rich and the family will love it!

Italian Dinner

2 pounds lean ground round beef
1 onion, chopped
1 sweet red bell pepper, chopped
2 ribs celery, chopped
2 garlic cloves, finely minced
1 (32 ounce) jar spaghetti sauce
3 (6 ounce) jars sliced mushrooms, drained
½ teaspoon ground oregano
1 teaspoon Italian seasoning
Salt and pepper
1 (8 ounce) package medium egg noodles
1 (8 ounce) package cream cheese, softened
1 pint carton sour cream
1 cup grated parmesan cheese
1 (16 ounce) package shredded mozzarella cheese

- In very large skillet, brown beef, onion, bell pepper, celery and garlic and drain well.
- Add spaghetti sauce, mushrooms and seasonings. Heat to boiling, turn heat down and simmer for about 15 minutes.
- Cook noodles according to package directions and drain.
- With electric mixer, beat cream cheese until creamy and add sour cream and cheeses.
- Butter deep 11 x 14-inch baking dish. Layer half the noodles, half the beef mixture and half the cheeses. Repeat layers.
- Bake covered at 325° for 30 minutes. Remove covering and bake another 10 to 15 minutes.

Baked Italian dishes are famous for their rich flavorful sauces. This recipe tastes wonderful on the first night and is even better the next day served as leftovers.

Simple Spaghetti Bake

8 ounces spaghetti
1 pound lean ground beef
1 green bell pepper, finely chopped
1 onion, chopped
1 (10 ounce) can tomato bisque soup
1 (15 ounce) can tomato sauce
⅓ cup water
½ teaspoon salt
2 teaspoons Italian seasoning
1 (8 ounce) can whole kernel corn, drained
1 (4 ounce) can black sliced olives, drained
1 (12 ounce) package shredded cheddar cheese

- Cook spaghetti according to package directions, drain and set aside.
- In skillet cook beef, bell pepper and onion and drain.
- Add remaining ingredients and spaghetti to beef mixture and stir well. Pour into greased 9 x 13-inch baking dish and cover.
- Refrigerate 2 to 3 hours.
- Bake covered at 350° for 45 minutes.

Casserole Beef Stew

1 (2-3 pound) chuck roast, cut in bite-size pieces
2 tablespoons oil
1 cup sliced carrots
2 onions, chopped
4 potatoes, peeled, cubed
1 cup chopped celery
2 teaspoons seasoned salt
1 teaspoon pepper
1 (10 ½ ounce) can golden mushroom soup
½ cup water
½ cup burgundy wine

- In large skillet brown pieces of roast in oil.
- Place in large sprayed roasting pan.
- Add all remaining ingredients.
- Cover and bake at 300° for 5 hours.

Company Beef and Pasta

2 pounds lean, ground beef
2 onions, chopped
1 green bell pepper, chopped
¾ teaspoon garlic powder
1 (14 ounce) jar spaghetti sauce
1 (15 ounce) can Italian stewed tomatoes
1 (4 ounce) can sliced mushrooms, drained
1 (8 ounce) package rotini pasta, divided
1 ½ pints sour cream, divided
1 (8 ounce) package sliced provolone cheese
1 (8 ounce) package shredded mozzarella cheese

- In deep skillet or kettle, brown and cook beef, stirring often to break up pieces. Drain off excess fat.
- Add onions, bell pepper, garlic powder, spaghetti sauce, stewed tomatoes and mushrooms and mix well. Simmer 20 minutes.
- Cook rotini according to package directions and drain. Pour half the rotini into buttered deep 11 x 14-inch baking dish.
- Cover with half the meat-tomato mixture and half the sour cream. Top with slices of provolone cheese. Repeat process once more ending with mozzarella cheese.
- Cover and bake at 325° for 35 minutes.
- Remove cover and continue baking another 10 to15 minutes or until mozzarella cheese melts.

Fettuccine Italian

6 ounces uncooked fettuccini
½ pound lean ground beef
1 teaspoon minced garlic
1 onion, minced
1 (8 ounce) can tomato sauce
1 (15 ounce) can Italian stewed tomatoes, undrained
1 teaspoon Italian seasoning
2 eggs, divided
2 tablespoons butter
1 (8 ounce) package shredded mozzarella cheese
1 (8 ounce) carton small curd cottage cheese, drained
1 cup chopped fresh broccoli, stemmed
1 (3 ounce) package grated parmesan cheese

- Cook fettuccine according to package directions, drain and set aside.
- In large skillet, brown beef and stir to crumble. Add garlic and onion, stir to mix and reduce heat. Cook for 5 minutes.
- Add tomato sauce, stewed tomatoes with liquid and Italian seasoning. Stir and bring to a boil. Reduce heat, cover and simmer for 10 to 12 minutes, stirring occasionally.
- Beat 1 egg and melted butter in mixing bowl. Stir in fettuccine and mozzarella cheese.
- Spoon mixture into ungreased, deep 10-inch pie plate and press down on bottom and sides of plate to pack fettuccine mixture.
- Mix remaining egg and cottage cheese in separate bowl. Pour over fettuccine in pie plate and smooth over surface. Sprinkle with broccoli.
- Spoon beef mixture evenly over top. Sprinkle parmesan evenly over top and remove any cheese from edges of the pie plate.
- Bake uncovered at 350° for 30 minutes or until thoroughly hot. Let stand 10 minutes to set before cutting.

Adding broccoli to this classic Italian recipe
dresses it up and adds wonderful flavor.

Cheesy Stuffed Bell Peppers

6 green bell peppers
1 ½ pounds lean ground beef
½ cup chopped onion
¾ cup cooked rice
1 egg
2 (15 ounce) cans Italian stewed tomatoes, divided
1 teaspoon seasoned salt
½ teaspoon black pepper
½ teaspoon garlic powder
1 tablespoon worcestershire sauce
1 (8 ounce) package shredded cheddar cheese, divided

- Cut off small portion of tops of bell pepper and remove seeds and membranes. Place in roaster with salted water and boil. Cook 10 minutes so they will be only partially done. Drain and set aside to cool.
- In skillet, brown ground beef and onion and drain. Add rice, egg, 1 can tomatoes, worcestershire and seasonings. Simmer 5 minutes.
- Remove from heat and add 1 cup cheese and mix well.
- Stuff peppers with mixture and set upright in buttered, round baking dish. (You may have to trim little slivers off bottoms of peppers so they will sit upright.)
- Pour remaining can of tomatoes over top and around peppers.
- Bake uncovered at 350° for 25 minutes.
- Remove from oven and sprinkle remaining cheese on top and return to oven for 10 minutes.

Stuffed peppers have to be a "down-home" special supper! In just about every casserole we make, we use bell peppers, but with this recipe you get the whole pepper with just the right "stuff" to make it delicious.

Easy Winter Warmer

1 (12 ounce) package medium egg noodles
3 tablespoons butter
1 ½ pounds lean ground round beef
1 (10 ounce) package frozen Seasoning Blend
(chopped onions and peppers), thawed
1 (28 ounce) jar spaghetti sauce
1 (12 ounce) package shredded mozzarella cheese

- In pot of boiling water with a dab of oil and salt, cook noodles according to package directions. Drain thoroughly, add butter and stir until butter melts.
- Brown beef and onions and peppers and drain thoroughly.
- Pour half of spaghetti sauce in bottom of buttered 9 x 13-inch baking dish.
- Layer half noodles, half the beef and half of the cheese. Repeat for a second layer.
- Bake covered at 350° for about 30 minutes or until dish is heated thoroughly.

This is such a good spaghetti sauce on noodles and is a great substitute for cream sauce.

Super Spaghetti Pie

6 ounces spaghetti
⅓ cup grated parmesan cheese
1 egg, beaten
1 tablespoon margarine, melted
1 cup small curd cottage cheese, drained
½ pound lean ground beef
½ pound sausage
½ cup chopped onion
1 (15 ounce) can tomato sauce
1 teaspoon garlic powder
1 tablespoon sugar
½ teaspoon salt
½ teaspoon seasoned pepper
1 teaspoon oregano
½ cup shredded mozzarella cheese

- Cook spaghetti according to package directions. While spaghetti is still warm, stir in parmesan cheese, egg and margarine in large bowl.
- Pour into well greased 10-inch pie plate and pat mixture up and around sides with a spoon to form a crust.
- Spoon cottage cheese over spaghetti crust.
- In skillet brown ground meat, sausage and onion. Drain off fat and add tomato sauce and seasonings. Simmer 10 minutes, stirring occasionally.
- Spoon meat mixture over cottage cheese.
- Bake at 350° for 30 minutes.
- Arrange mozzarella on top and return to oven just until cheese melts.

This is a great recipe to make ahead of time and have ready for a late supper after the game or a midnight supper when teen-agers demand "food"! What better than "food" that resembles pizza?

Pepper Steak

1 ½ pounds boneless sirloin, ¾-inch thick
3 tablespoons oil
1 green bell pepper, julienned
1 sweet red bell pepper, julienned
1 onion, cut in wedges
1 teaspoon minced garlic
1 (14 ounce) can beef broth
2 tablespoons cornstarch
1 (10 ounce) can beefy mushroom soup
2 tablespoons soy sauce
½ teaspoon ground ginger
½ teaspoon salt
4 cups hot cooked, white rice

- Slice beef across the grain into thin strips. Pour oil in large skillet and brown steak on high heat. Reduce heat and cook on low for 10 minutes.
- With a slotted spoon, place beef in 3-quart baking dish.
- Saute bell peppers, onion and garlic in skillet with remaining oil. Combine beef broth and cornstarch and mix well.
- Stir in beef broth, soup, soy sauce, ginger and salt and heat to boiling.
- Pour soup mixture over beef, cover and bake at 350° for about 65 minutes. Serve over hot rice.

*You can't beat this tender sirloin and colorful peppers
with a tasty beef sauce.*

Round Steak Casserole

2 pounds lean round steak, tenderized
Seasoned salt
Seasoned pepper
3 tablespoons oil
1 onion, chopped
1 cup uncooked rice
1 (14 ounce) can beef broth
1 can plus ⅓ cup water
1 tablespoon dried parsley flakes
½ teaspoon garlic powder
¼ teaspoon salt
2 tablespoons worcestershire sauce
1 green bell pepper, julienned
1 sweet red bell pepper, julienned
1 (7 ounce) can chopped green chilies, optional

- Trim fat off edges of steak and cut into serving-size pieces. Season with seasoned salt and pepper.
- Pour oil in large skillet and brown steak on both sides. Remove to greased 9 x 13-inch baking dish.
- In bowl, combine onion, rice, beef broth, water, parsley flakes, garlic powder, salt, worcestershire, bell peppers and green chilies. Spoon over steak.
- Cover and bake at 350° for 45 minutes.

This is definitely not a luncheon dish. The men are going to call for this "beef" over and over again.

Flank Steak Royal

2 (1 ½ pound each) beef flank steaks
1 (6 ounce) jar marinated artichoke hearts, drained, chopped
2 bunches fresh green onions and tops, finely chopped
1 pound bacon, fried, drained, crumbled
1 ½ cups soft breadcrumbs
1 ½ cups grated romano cheese
2 cups very finely chopped fresh spinach
worcestershire sauce
2 teaspoons minced garlic
½ cup (1 stick) margarine
½ pound fresh mushrooms, sliced
1 onion, sliced
2 tablespoons dried parsley
2 (14 ounce) cans beef broth
2 cups instant brown rice, cooked

- Tenderize flank steaks twice or ask butcher to tenderize.
- In large bowl, combine artichoke hearts, onions, crispy bacon, breadcrumbs, romano cheese and very finely chopped fresh spinach and toss thoroughly.
- Divide mixture in half and pat evenly over flank steaks. Carefully roll each steak in jelly-roll fashion. With a cotton twine, tie securely in 6 to 8 places and seal ends securely.
- Rub steak with worcesterhire and minced garlic.
- Drop butter in large skillet on medium low heat and sear meat on all sides until brown. Place in large roasting pan.

(Continued on next page.)

- In medium bowl, mix sliced mushrooms, chopped onion, parsley and beef broth and mix well.
- Pour over steak rolls, cover and cook at 325° for 1 hour or until fork tender.
- Remove cover and cook another 10 minutes for steak to brown slightly. Remove from pan and allow to stand for about 10 minutes before slicing in about ¾-inch slices.
- Arrange rice on large platter and place sliced steak over rice. Use remaining broth as a sauce to serve with steak and rice.

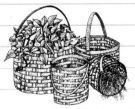

Best Pot Roast Dinner

4 pound boneless rump roast
Seasoned salt
Seasoned pepper
Garlic powder
1 ½ cups water
6 potatoes, peeled, quartered
8 carrots, peeled, quartered
3 onions, peeled, quartered

Gravy:
3 tablespoons cornstarch
¾ cup water
½ teaspoon black pepper
½ teaspoon salt

- Set roast in roasting pan with lid and sprinkle liberally with seasoned salt, pepper and garlic powder. Add 1 ½ cups water and cook covered at 375° for about 30 minutes.
- Turn heat down to 325° and cook for about 2 ½ to 3 hours or until roast is fork tender.
- Add potatoes, carrots and onions. Cook another 35 to 40 minutes.
- To make gravy, lift roast out of roaster and place on serving platter.
- Place potatoes, carrots and onions around roast.
- Combine cornstarch and water and add to juices left in roaster. Add pepper and salt.
- Cook on high on top of stove until gravy thickens, stirring constantly. Serve in gravy boat with roast and vegetables.

Well, we can't really say this is a casserole, but if you stretch your imagination, it is because you have your whole meal cooked in one container and everybody loves pot roast.

Ravioli and More

1 pound lean ground beef
½ teaspoon seasoned salt
1 teaspoon garlic powder
½ teaspoon black pepper
1 large onion, chopped
2 grated zucchini squash
¼ cup (½ stick) margarine
1 (28 ounce) jar spaghetti sauce
1 (25 ounce) package ravioli with portobello mushrooms,
cooked
1 (12 ounce) package shredded mozzarella cheese

- In large skillet brown ground beef until no longer pink and drain. Add salt, garlic powder and pepper.
- In saucepan cook onion and zucchini in margarine just until tender-crisp and stir in spaghetti sauce.
- In buttered 9 x 13-inch baking dish, spread ½ cup sauce. Layer half of ravioli, half spaghetti sauce, half beef and half cheese. Repeat the layers, omitting the remaining cheese. Cover and bake at 350° for 35 minutes.
- Uncover and sprinkle remaining cheese. Let stand 10 minutes before serving.

Beef

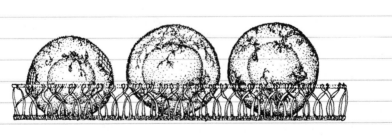

Sombrero Ole

1 (1 ½ pound) package lean ground beef
1 teaspoon seasoning salt
1 large onion, chopped
1 red bell pepper, chopped
1 yellow bell pepper, chopped
3 cups chopped zucchini
½-¾ cup water
1 envelope taco seasoning
1 cup uncooked rice
1 teaspoon salt
1 (16 ounce) jar chunky salsa
1 ½ cups grated cheddar cheese
2 cups lightly crushed tortilla chips

- In large skillet brown ground beef, drain and add seasoning salt.
- Add onion, bell peppers, zucchini, water and taco seasoning. Stir and sauté until vegetables are tender.
- In separate saucepan, cook rice according to directions.
- In sprayed 9 x 13-inch baking dish, spoon rice over bottom of dish and layer beef mixture, salsa and cheese.
- Bake at 350° for 20 to 25 minutes.
- Remove from oven and sprinkle tortilla chips over top. Bake for another 10 minutes.

Pork
Casseroles

Pork Chop Cheddar Bake

8 boneless pork chops
1 (10 ounce) can cream of mushroom soup
1 ¼ cups water
1 cup uncooked rice
1 ½ cups grated cheddar cheese, divided
½ cup minced onion
⅓ cup chopped bell pepper
1 (4 ounce) can sliced mushrooms, drained
1 can french-fried onions

- In large skillet, brown pork chops lightly. Drain and place in greased 9 x 13-inch baking dish.
- In same skillet, combine soup, water, rice, ½ cup cheese, onion, bell pepper and mushrooms and mix well. Pour over pork chops.
- Cover with foil and bake at 325° for 1 hour and 10 minutes.
- Uncover and top with remaining cheese and french-fried onions. Return to oven just until cheese melts.

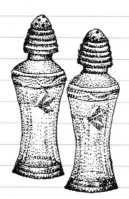

Apricot Pork Chops

1 (15 ounce) can apricot halves, undrained
8 (½-inch thick) boneless pork chops
3 tablespoons margarine
⅓ cup chopped celery
1 yellow bell pepper, chopped
2 ½ cups uncooked instant rice
¾ cup hot water
1 teaspoon chicken bouillon
⅓ cup golden raisins
½ teaspoon ground ginger
½ teaspoon salt
½ cup slivered almonds

- Place apricots in food processor, cover and process until smooth. Set aside.
- In skillet, brown pork chops on both sides in margarine, reduce heat and simmer for about 10 minutes. Remove pork chops to a heated plate.
- In same skillet, saute celery and bell pepper and add rice, water, bouillon, raisins, ginger, salt and apricot puree and bring to a boil.
- Remove from heat and stir in almonds. Spoon into 9 x 13-inch baking dish.
- Place pork chops on top of rice mixture.
- Cover and bake at 350° for 20 minutes.

Pork Chops and Apples

6 (¾-inch) bone-in pork chops
¼ cup (½ stick) margarine, divided
6 cups stuffing croutons
1 cup peeled, chopped green apples
½ cup chopped celery
½ cup golden raisins
½ cup chopped pecans
½ cup hot water
2 teaspoons rubbed sage
1 teaspoon seasoned salt
1 tablespoon Dijon mustard

- In large skillet, brown pork chops on both sides in 2 tablespoons margarine and set aside.
- In same skillet, melt remaining margarine, stir in croutons, chopped apples, celery, raisins, pecans, water, sage and salt and mix well.
- Place crouton mixture into greased 7 x 11-inch baking dish. Top with pork chops.
- Spread a thin layer of mustard over each pork chop. Cover and bake at 325° for 40 minutes.
- Uncover and bake another 10 minutes.

Pork Chop Casserole

6 (¾-inch) boneless pork chops
½ teaspoon seasoned salt
½ teaspoon pepper
2 tablespoons oil
1 green bell pepper
1 yellow bell pepper, seeded, chopped
1 (15 ounce) can tomato sauce
1 (15 ounce) can Italian stewed tomatoes, undrained
1 cup water
1 teaspoon minced garlic
½ teaspoon salt
1 ½ cups uncooked long grain rice

- Sprinkle pork chops with salt and pepper. In skillet, brown pork chops in oil. Remove chops from skillet and set aside.
- Cut top off green pepper, remove seeds and cut 6 rings from green bell pepper and set aside.
- In separate bowl, combine chopped yellow pepper, tomato sauce, Italian stewed tomatoes, water, garlic and salt and stir well.
- Spread rice in greased 9 x 13-inch baking dish and slowly pour tomato mixture over rice.
- Arrange pork chops over rice and place pepper ring over each chop.
- Cover and bake at 350° for 1 hour or until chops and rice are tender.

Orange Pork Chops

6 (½-inch) boneless pork chops
Salt and pepper
2 tablespoons oil
1 ⅓ cups uncooked instant rice
1 cup orange juice
¼ teaspoon ground ginger
1 (10 ounce) can condensed chicken with rice soup,
undiluted
½ cup chopped walnuts

- Sprinkle salt and pepper over pork chops and brown in skillet with oil.
- Sprinkle rice into greased 7 x 11-inch baking dish. Add orange juice and arrange pork chops over rice.
- Add ginger to soup and stir right in can. Pour soup over pork chops.
- Sprinkle walnuts over tops of pork chops.
- Cover and bake at 350° for 25 minutes.
- Uncover and bake 10 minutes longer or until rice is tender.

Italian-Style Pork Chops

6 (¾-inch) bone-in pork chops
Salt and pepper
2 tablespoons oil
2 green bell peppers
1 (15 ounce) can tomato sauce
1 (15 ounce) can Italian-style stewed tomatoes, undrained
1 cup water
½ onion, chopped
1 teaspoon Italian seasoning
½ teaspoon salt
½ teaspoon pepper
1 clove garlic, minced
1 tablespoon worchestershire sauce
½ cup uncooked brown rice

- Sprinkle pork chops with a little salt and pepper. In skillet, brown chops on both sides in oil. Remove chops from skillet, drain and set aside.
- Cut top off 1 bell pepper and remove seeds. Cut 6 (¼-inch thick) rings from 1 bell pepper and set aside. Seed and chop remaining bell pepper.
- Combine chopped bell pepper, tomato sauce, stewed tomatoes, water, onion, Italian seasoning, salt, pepper, garlic and worcestershire and mix well.
- Spread rice evenly in lightly greased 9 x 13-inch baking pan. Slowly pour tomato mixture over rice.
- Arrange pork chops over rice mixture and top each pork chop with a pepper ring.
- Bake covered at 350° for 1 hour or until rice is tender.

Pepperoni Twirls

2 cups tomato-spinach macaroni twirls
1 pound bulk Italian sausage
1 onion, chopped
1 green bell pepper, chopped
1 (15 ounce) can pizza sauce
1 (8 ounce) can tomato sauce
⅓ cup milk
1 (3 ½-ounce) package sliced pepperoni, halved
1 (4 ounce) jar sliced mushrooms, drained
1 (2 ounce) can sliced ripe olives, drained
1 (8 ounce) package shredded mozzarella cheese, divided

- Cook macaroni twirls according to package directions and drain.
- In skillet over medium heat, cook sausage, onion and bell pepper until sausage is no longer pink and drain.
- In large bowl, combine pizza sauce, tomato sauce and milk. Stir in sausage mixture, macaroni twirls, pepperoni, mushrooms, olives and half the cheese and mix well.
- Spoon into greased 9 x 13-inch baking dish. Cover and bake at 350° for 30 minutes.
- Remove from oven and sprinkle remaining cheese over top of casserole and return to oven for 5-10 minutes or just until cheese melts.

Pork

Zesty Ziti

1 pound Italian sausage links, cut into ½-inch chunks
1 onion, coarsely chopped
1 green bell pepper, julienned
1 tablespoon oil
1 (15 ounce) can diced tomatoes
1 (15 ounce) can Italian stewed tomatoes
2 tablespoons ketchup
1 (16 ounce) package ziti pasta
1 cup shredded mozzarella cheese

- Cook sausage, onion and bell pepper in oil over medium heat in large skillet and drain.
- Add diced tomatoes, stewed tomatoes and ketchup and mix well.
- Cook ziti according to package directions and drain.
- In large bowl, combine sausage-tomato mixture and toss with pasta and cheese.
- Spoon into greased 3-quart baking dish. Cover and bake at 350° from 20 minutes.

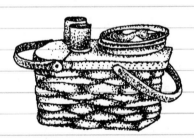

Pork-Stuffed Eggplant

1 large eggplant
¾ pound ground pork
½ pound pork sausage
1 egg
½ cup dry breadcrumbs
½ cup grated romano cheese
1 tablespoon dried parsley flakes
1 tablespoon dried onion flakes
1 teaspoon dried oregano
½ teaspoon salt
½ teaspoon pepper
1 (15 ounce) can stewed tomatoes
1 (8 ounce) can tomato sauce

- Cut off eggplant stem and cut in half lengthwise. Scoop out and reserve center, leaving a ½-inch shell.
- Steam shell halves for about 5 minutes or just until tender. Drain well.
- Cube reserved eggplant and cook in saucepan with boiling salted water for about 6 minutes, drain well and set aside.
- In skillet over medium heat, cook pork and sausage until no longer pink and drain.
- Add eggplant cubes, egg, breadcrumbs, cheese, parsley flakes, onion flakes, oregano, salt and pepper and mix well.
- Fill shells and place in greased 7 x 11-inch baking dish. Pour stewed tomatoes and tomato sauce over eggplant.
- Cover and bake at 350° for 30 minutes.

Pork

Pork Loin with Fruit Sauce

1 (4 pound) pork loin roast
1 teaspoon dried rosemary
1 teaspoon seasoned pepper
⅛ cup (¼ stick) margarine
1 cup orange juice
1 (16 ounce) can whole berry cranberry sauce
1 cup apricot preserves
1 (14 ounce) can chicken broth
1 teaspoon red wine vinegar
1 teaspoon sugar
1 teaspoon salt
1 tablespoon white wine worcestershire sauce
Cooked white rice

- Place roast in shallow roasting pan. Sprinkle roast with rosemary and pepper.
- Bake uncovered at 350° for 1 hour.
- In large saucepan, combine remaining ingredients. Bring ingredients to a boiling point, reduce heat and simmer for 20 minutes.
- Remove roast from oven and spoon about 1 cup sauce over roast. Return to oven and cook another hour or until meat thermometer reads 165°. Let roast stand several minutes before slicing.
- Spoon meat juices from roast into fruit sauce. Heat and serve with pork roast. Serve over hot cooked rice.

Pork

Fiesta Pork Casserole

2 pounds boneless pork tenderloin, cut into 1-inch cubes
1 onion, chopped
1 green bell pepper, chopped
3 tablespoons oil
1 (15 ounce) can black beans, rinsed, drained
1 (10 ounce) can fiesta nacho cheese
1 (15 ounce) can stewed tomatoes
1 (4 ounce) can chopped green chilies
1 cup instant brown rice, cooked
¾ cup salsa
2 teaspoons ground cumin
½ teaspoon salt
½ teaspoon garlic powder
1 cup shredded Mexican 3-cheese blend

- In very large skillet or roasting pan, brown and cook pork, onion and bell pepper in oil until pork is no longer pink. Drain.
- Add beans, fiesta nacho cheese soup, stewed tomatoes, green chilies, rice, salsa, cumin, salt and garlic powder. Cook on medium heat, stirring occasionally, until mixture is bubbly.
- Spoon into buttered 4-quart baking dish. Bake uncovered at 350° for 30 minutes or until bubbly around the edges.
- Remove from oven and sprinkle with cheese. Let stand a few minutes before serving.

This zesty casserole is so easy to put together and it really gets your attention! It is a specially nice change of pace from the usual Mexican dish with ground beef.

One-Dish Pork and Peas

1-1 ½ pounds pork tenderloin, cut into ½-inch cubes
2 tablespoons oil
1 cup sliced celery
1 onion, chopped
1 sweet red bell pepper, chopped
1 (8 ounce) package small egg noodles, cooked, drained
1 (10 ounce) can cream of chicken soup
½ cup half-and-half cream
1 (10 ounce) package frozen green peas, thawed
1 teaspoon seasoned salt
½ teaspoon black pepper
1 cup seasoned dry breadcrumbs
⅓ cup chopped walnuts

- In large skillet, brown cubed pork in oil. Reduce heat and cook for about 20 minutes. Remove pork to a separate dish.
- In remaining oil saute celery, onion and bell pepper.
- Add pork, noodles, soup, cream, peas, salt and pepper.
- Spoon into buttered 3-quart baking dish. Sprinkle with breadcrumbs and walnuts.
- Bake uncovered at 350° for about 25 minutes or until bubbly.

So many of our casseroles are chicken, but pork is so good and always tender. This blend of ingredients makes a delicious dish.

Tenderloin and Peppers

1 pork tenderloin, thinly sliced
Olive oil
1 sweet red bell pepper, julienned
1 green bell pepper, julienned
½ pound fresh mushrooms, quartered
1 onion, coarsely chopped
1 teaspoon minced garlic
½ cup beef broth
2 tablespoons ketchup
1 teaspoon lemon juice
1 teaspoon dried tarragon
½ teaspoon black pepper
1 tablespoon flour
½ cup sour cream
Cooked noodles

- In large skillet, brown pork slices in a little olive oil. Remove and keep warm.
- In same skillet, saute peppers, mushrooms, onion and garlic in a little more oil.
- Add broth, ketchup, lemon juice, tarragon and black pepper. Simmer uncovered for 3 minutes. Return pork to skillet.
- Combine flour with sour cream and stir into pork mixture. Spoon into greased 7 x 11-inch baking dish.
- Cover and cook at 325° for 20 minutes. Serve over hot cooked noodles.

Pork and Noodles Supreme

2 tablespoons oil

2 pounds pork tenderloin, cut into 1-inch cubes

2 ribs celery, chopped

1 sweet red bell pepper, chopped

1 green bell pepper, chopped

1 onion, chopped

1 (12 ounce) package medium egg noodles, cooked, drained

1 (10 ounce) can cream of celery soup

1 (10 ounce) can cream of chicken soup

1 (15 ounce) can creamed corn

¾ cup half-and-half cream

1 teaspoon salt

1 teaspoon black pepper

1 ½ cups crushed corn flakes

3 tablespoons margarine, melted

- In skillet, heat oil and brown and cook pork about 15 minutes. Spoon pork into a large bowl.
- With remaining oil in skillet, saute celery, bell pepper and onion. Spoon into the bowl with pork. Add noodles, both soups, creamed corn, half-and-half, salt and pepper to pork.
- Mix well and pour into buttered 9 x 13-inch baking dish.
- Combine crushed corn flakes and margarine and sprinkle over casserole. Bake covered at 350° for about 30 minutes.

Oodles of Noodles

1 ½-2 pounds pork tenderloin, cut into 1-inch cubes
3 tablespoons oil
2 cups chopped celery
1 sweet red bell pepper, chopped
1 green bell pepper, chopped
1 onion, chopped
1 (4 ounce) can sliced mushrooms
1 (10 ounce) can tomatoes and green chilies
1 (10 ounce) can cream of mushroom soup with garlic
1 (10 ounce) can cream of celery soup
¼ cup soy sauce
1 (7 ounce) package elbow macaroni, cooked, drained
2 cups chow mein noodles

- In skillet, brown pork in oil and cook on low heat for about 15 minutes. Remove pork with slotted spoon to a side dish.
- Saute celery, bell peppers and onion in same skillet in remaining oil. In large bowl, combine pork, celery-onion mixture, mushrooms, tomatoes and green chilies, soups, soy sauce and macaroni.
- Spoon ingredients into one large, buttered 9 x 13-inch baking dish or 2 smaller baking dishes. Top with chow mein noodles.
- Bake uncovered at 350° for 50 minutes.

If you make 2 smaller casseroles, you may freeze one. Wait to sprinkle the chow mein noodles over casserole until just before you place it in the oven to cook.

Ham and Potatoes Ole!

1 (24 ounce) package frozen hash browns with onion and
peppers, thawed
3 cups cubed, cooked ham
1 (10 ounce) can cream of chicken soup
1 (10 ounce) can fiesta nacho cheese soup
1 cup hot salsa
1 (8 ounce) package shredded cheddar-jack cheese

- In large bowl, combine potatoes, ham, both soups and salsa and
  mix well.
- Spoon into buttered 9 x 13-inch baking dish.
- Cover and cook at 350° for 40 minutes.
- Remove from oven, sprinkle cheese over casserole and bake
  uncovered another 5 minutes.

Noodles and Ham
With Veggies

1 (8 ounce) package medium egg noodles
1 (10 ounce) can cream of celery soup, undiluted
1 (10 ounce) can cream of broccoli soup, undiluted
1 teaspoon chicken bouillon
1 ½ cups half-and-half cream
1 (8 ounce) can whole kernel corn, drained
1 (16 ounce) package frozen broccoli, cauliflower and carrots, thawed
3 cups cooked cubed ham
½ teaspoon seasoned salt
1 teaspoon white pepper
1 (8 ounce) package shredded cheddar-jack cheese, divided

- Cook noodles according to package directions and drain.
- In large bowl, combine soups, chicken bouillon, cream, corn, broccoli-carrot mixture, ham, salt and pepper and mix well.
- Fold in egg noodles and half of cheese.
- Spoon into greased 9 x 13-inch baking dish. Cover and bake at 350° for 45 minutes.
- Uncover and sprinkle remaining cheese over top of casserole. Return to oven and bake another 10 minutes or until cheese is bubbly.

Pork

Ham-it Up
With Wild Rice

1 (6.2 ounce) package instant long grain, wild rice
1 (10 ounce) package frozen broccoli spears, thawed
1 (8 ounce) can whole kernel corn, drained
3 cups cubed, fully cooked ham
1 (10 ounce) can cream of mushroom soup
1 cup mayonnaise
1 teaspoon prepared mustard
½ teaspoon seasoned salt
½ teaspoon black pepper
1 cup shredded cheddar cheese
1 (2.8 ounce) can fried onion rings

- Prepare rice according to package directions.
- Spoon into buttered 3-quart baking dish. Top with broccoli, corn and ham.
- In saucepan, combine soup, mayonnaise, mustard, seasoned salt, pepper and shredded cheese and mix well. Spread over top of rice-ham mixture.
- Cover and bake at 350° for about 30 minutes. Remove from oven and sprinkle onion rings over top.
- Return to oven, uncovered, and bake another 15 minutes or until casserole is bubbly around edges and onion rings are lightly browned.

What a great way to use left-over ham, all the little slivers and chunks left from those nice big slices. It is really simple to put together and the kids will be ready to eat their vegetables when it has ham and cheese to compliment them.

Walnut-Ham Linguine

2 teaspoons minced garlic
½ cup coarsely chopped walnuts
1 sweet red bell pepper, julienned
¼ cup olive oil
½ pound cooked ham, cut in strips
1 (16 ounce) jar creamy alfredo sauce
¼ cup grated parmesan cheese
1 (12 ounce) package linguine, cooked al dente
1 cup seasoned breadcrumbs

- In large skillet, saute garlic, walnuts and bell pepper in oil for 1 to 2 minutes.
- In large bowl, combine garlic-bell pepper mixture, ham, alfredo sauce, parmesan cheese and linguine and mix well.
- Spoon into buttered 3-quart casserole dish. Sprinkle breadcrumbs over top.
- Bake uncovered at 350° for 35 minutes or until breadcrumbs are lightly browned.

Pork

Sandwich Souffle

Margarine, softened
8 slices white bread, crusts removed
4 slices ham
4 slices American cheese
2 cups milk
2 eggs, beaten
Salt and pepper

- Butter bread on both sides, make 4 sandwiches with ham and cheese.
- Place sandwiches in buttered 8-inch square baking pan,
- Beat together milk, eggs and a little salt and pepper. Pour over sandwiches and soak for 1 to 2 hours.
- Bake at 375° for 45 to 50 minutes.

A fun lunch!

Ham and Cheese Bars

2 cups Bisquick
1 heaping cup cooked, finely chopped ham
1 cup shredded cheddar cheese
½ onion, finely chopped
½ cup grated parmesan cheese
¼ cup sour cream
½ teaspoon salt
1 teaspoon garlic powder
1 cup whole milk
1 egg

- In a bowl, combine all ingredients in a mixing bowl and mix by hand.
- Spread in a greased 9 x 13 inch baking pan.
- Bake at 350° for 30 minutes or until lightly brown.
- Cut in rectangles, about 2 inches by 1 inch. Serve hot or room temperature.

This is not exactly a casserole, but it goes well with a lot of our brunch casseroles. They can be served at brunch or lunch and they can be kept in the refrigerator (cooked) and reheated. To reheat, bake at 325° for about 15 minutes. They will be good and crispy when reheated.

Spectacular Ham-Asparagus Casserole

½ cup slivered almonds
2 tablespoons butter
½ cup seasoned breadcrumbs
1 pound fresh asparagus, trimmed
2 cups cooked, cubed ham
½ cup grated cheddar cheese
3 tablespoons tapioca
3 tablespoons chopped green onions and tops
½ cup chopped mushrooms
3 tablespoons minced red bell pepper
2 tablespoons fresh, snipped parsley
1 tablespoon lemon juice
4 hard-boiled eggs, divided
½ cup milk
1 (10 ounce) cream of mushroom soup
Paprika

- Pour almond slivers onto baking sheet and toast at 250° for 10 to 15 minutes. Remove and set aside to cool.
- In saucepan, melt butter and remove from heat. Add breadcrumbs and toss to coat. Set aside.
- Arrange fresh asparagus in steamer basket and cook in saucepan of water for about 2 to 3 minutes until slightly tender.
- Drain, arrange asparagus in sprayed 1½ -quart baking dish and set aside.
- In mixing bowl stir together ham, cheddar cheese, tapioca, onion, mushrooms, almonds, bell pepper, parsley and lemon juice until well mixed.
- Carefully slice eggs into thin, diagonal pieces.
- Spoon a layer of half the ham mixture over asparagus and top with layer of half the egg slices. Repeat layers with remaining ham mixture and remaining egg slices.
- In mixing bowl pour milk into mushroom soup and whisk until well blended. Slowly pour over ham mixture in baking dish.
- Top with breadcrumbs and small sprinkles of paprika.
- Bake at 350° for 25 to 30 minutes.

Old-Fashioned Ham Loaf With Sassy Horseradish Sauce

3 eggs
3 pounds lean ground ham
3 cups soft, fine breadcrumbs
2 teaspoons brown sugar
2 teaspoons prepared horseradish

Horseradish Sauce:
1 teaspoon prepared horseradish
⅛ teaspoon salt
½ pint whipping cream

- Slightly beat eggs in large mixing bowl.
- Stir in ground ham and mix thoroughly.
- Add breadcrumbs, brown sugar and horseradish and stir to mix well.
- Form into a loaf and put in a sprayed baking dish.
- Bake at 350° for 1½ hours.
- Mix all sauce ingredients and chill. Allow sauce to reach room temperature 20 minutes before serving.
- Remove loaf from oven, allow to set for about 5 minutes before slicing. Serve with sauce.

Seafood Casseroles

Roughy Florentine

3 tablespoons butter
2 (10 ounce) boxes frozen spinach, thawed, drained
½ teaspoon seasoned salt
½ teaspoon black pepper
⅛ teaspoon ground nutmeg
2 pounds orange roughy fillets
5 tablespoon (⅔ stick) butter
⅓ cup minced onion
1 envelope cream of spinach soup mix
1 pint half-and half-cream
2 cups shredded swiss cheese

- Heat 3 tablespoons butter in large skillet and cook spinach for about 2 minutes. Season with salt, pepper and nutmeg.
- Spoon spinach into buttered 9 x 13-inch baking dish and spread spinach over bottom of dish.
- Lay orange roughy over spinach.
- In saucepan heat butter and saute onion. Add soup mix, cream and cheese and mix well. Heat just until the cheese melts.
- Pour sauce over fillets and spinach.
- Cover and bake at 350° for 20 to 25 minutes or until the fillets flake easily and sauce is bubbly.

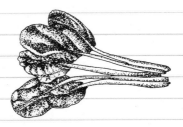

Crab-Stuffed Orange Roughy

⅓ cup seasoned breadcrumbs
1 egg, beaten
1 tablespoon finely minced onion
2 tablespoons finely minced sweet red bell pepper
1 teaspoon creole seasoning
1 teaspoon dry mustard
1 teaspoon dried parsley flakes
Scant teaspoon Tabasco
2 (6 ounce) cans crabmeat, drained, flaked, picked
8 (5 ounce) orange roughy fillets
3 tablespoons butter
2 tablespoons lemon juice
¼ teaspoon paprika
Commercial mornay sauce
Hot cooked rice

- In bowl, combine breadcrumbs, egg, onion, bell pepper, seasoning, mustard, parsley flakes and Tabasco and mix well. Add crabmeat and stir gently.
- Spoon ¼ cup crabmeat mixture onto each fillet. Roll up fillet to enclose filling. Place fillet rolls, seam-side down, in buttered 9 x 13-inch baking dish.
- Place a little dot of butter on each fillet and sprinkle with lemon juice and paprika.
- Bake uncovered at 350° for 30 minutes or until fish flakes easily when tested with a fork.
- Place rolls on bed of rice and serve with mornay sauce.
- (In case you cannot find the commercial mornay sauce use our recipe on the following page.)

Seafood

Mornay Sauce

1 tablespoon butter
1 tablespoon flour
1 cup milk
½ teaspoon seasoned salt
1 egg yolk, beaten
2 tablespoons whipping cream
3 tablespoons shredded Swiss cheese
2 tablespoons grated parmesan cheese

- Melt butter, add flour and cook about 1 minute, stirring constantly. Gradually add milk and salt and cook, stirring constantly, until mixture thickens.
- Combine egg yolk and whipping cream and very gradually add a little at a time to hot mixture, stirring constantly, until thick.
- Remove from heat and add cheeses, stirring until cheese melts.

Creamy Orange Roughy

½ cup (1 stick) butter, divided
1 sweet red bell pepper, chopped
1 onion, chopped
¼ cup flour
1 teaspoon basil
½ teaspoon white pepper
½ teaspoon salt
1 pint half-and-half cream
1 (3 ounce) package grated parmesan cheese
1 tablespoon white wine worcestershire
1 ½ pounds orange roughy fillets
3 hard-boiled eggs, sliced
1 ½ cups round buttery cracker crumbs

- In skillet, melt 4 tablespoons butter and saute bell pepper and onion.
- Add flour, basil, white pepper and salt to skillet and cook on medium heat about 2 minutes. Slowly add cream, stirring constantly until mixture thickens.
- Stir in parmesan cheese and white wine worcestershire.
- In another skillet, melt 2 tablespoons butter and brown orange roughy fillet. Transfer to greased 9 x 13-inch baking dish and place egg slices over fish.
- Pour cream sauce over eggs and fillets.
- Bake uncovered at 350° for 15 minutes.
- Combine cracker crumbs and remaining 2 tablespoons butter. Sprinkle crumbs over casserole and bake another 10 to 15 minutes or until crumbs are lightly browned.

You may substitute any white fish for the orange roughy.

Crabmeat Special

½ cup chopped celery
1 cup chopped onion
½ cup chopped red bell pepper
¼ cup (½ stick) margarine
2 tablespoons flour
1 pint half-and-half cream
1 egg, beaten
1 ½ teaspoons salt
2 ½ teaspoons Cajun seasoning
¼ teaspoon cayenne pepper
1 cup cooked white rice
1 pound fresh crabmeat, picked, shredded
1 cup shredded cheddar cheese

- In skillet, saute celery, onion and red bell pepper in margarine, but do not brown. Blend in flour over low heat.
- Gradually add cream, egg, salt, Cajun seasoning and cayenne pepper. Cook on medium heat, stirring constantly, about 5 minutes, until mixture thickens.
- Fold in rice and crabmeat and blend well. Spoon into buttered 2-quart casserole dish.
- Bake covered at 325° for 30 minutes or until bubbly. Uncover and sprinkle cheese over top of casserole.
- Return to oven for about 5 minutes, just until cheese melts.

The fresh crabmeat may be substituted for 2 (8 ounce) cartons Louis Kemp crab delights in refrigerated section of your grocery store.

"No Panic" Crab Casserole

2 (6 ounce) cans crabmeat, drained
1 cup half-and-half cream
1 ½ cups mayonnaise
6 hard-boiled eggs, finely chopped
1 cup seasoned breadcrumbs, divided
1 tablespoon dried parsley flakes
½ teaspoon dried basil
1 (8 ounce) can sliced water chestnuts, drained
½ teaspoon seasoned salt
¼ teaspoon white pepper
2 tablespoons margarine, melted

- In bowl, combine crabmeat, cream, mayonnaise, hard-boiled eggs, ½ cup seasoned breadcrumbs, parsley, basil, water chestnuts, salt and pepper and mix well. Pour into buttered 2-quart casserole dish.
- Combine remaining ½ cup breadcrumbs and margarine and sprinkle over top of casserole.
- Bake uncovered at 350° for 40 minutes.

Crab-Stuffed Baked Potatoes

4 large baking potatoes
½ cup (1 stick) butter
½ cup whipping cream
¾ teaspoon seasoned salt
½ teaspoon white pepper
1 bunch fresh green onions, chopped
2 (6 ounce) cans crabmeat, drained
¾ cup shredded cheddar cheese
2 tablespoons fresh minced parsley

- Bake potatoes at 375° for 1 hour or until well done. Halve each potato lengthwise and scoop out pulp, leaving skins intact.
- In large bowl, mash potatoes with butter. Add whipping cream, salt, pepper and green onions. Stir in crabmeat.
- Fill reserved potato skins with potato mixture. Sprinkle with the cheese.
- Bake at 350° for about 15 minutes.
- To serve, sprinkle fresh parsley over cheese.

*If you have been looking for a baked potato
that is truly a meal in itself, this is it!*

Seafood

Fettuccine of the Sea

¼ cup (½ stick) butter
¼ cup flour
1 teaspoon Creole seasoning
¾ teaspoon white pepper
1 tablespoon minced garlic
1 (16 ounce) carton half-and-half cream
½ cup milk
½ cup finely chopped red bell pepper
2 (6 ounce) cans tiny shrimp, picked, deveined
2 (6 ounce) cans crabmeat, picked, drained
1 (6 ounce) can chopped clams, drained
½ cup grated parmesan cheese
1 (12 ounce) package fettuccine, cooked al dente
Fresh parsley for topping

- In saucepan, melt butter and add flour, Creole seasoning, white pepper and garlic and mix well. On medium heat, gradually add cream and milk and mix well. Cook stirring constantly until thickened.
- Add bell pepper, shrimp, crabmeat, clams and parmesan cheese and heat thoroughly.
- In buttered 9 x 13-inch baking dish, spoon half fettuccine in bottom of dish and half seafood sauce. Repeat layers.
- Cover and bake at 325° for 25 minutes or just until casserole is bubbly. To serve, sprinkle parsley over top of casserole.

Seafood Lasagna

8 lasagna noodles

2 tablespoons margarine

1 onion, chopped

1 (8 ounce) package cream cheese, softened

1 (15 ounce) carton ricotta cheese

1 (4 ounce) jar chopped pimentos, drained

1 egg, beaten

2 teaspoons dried basil

½ teaspoon seasoned salt

½ teaspoon white pepper

1 (10 ounce) can cream of shrimp soup, undiluted

1 (10 ounce) can fiesta nacho cheese soup, undiluted

¼ cup milk

⅓ cup white wine

1 pound small, cooked shrimp, peeled, deveined

2 (6 ounce) cans crabmeat, drained

¼ cup grated parmesan cheese

1 cup shredded cheddar cheese

- Cook noodles according to package directions and set aside.
- In large skillet melt margarine and saute onion until tender, but do not brown. Stir in cream cheese, ricotta cheese, pimentos, egg, basil, seasoned salt and white pepper.
- In saucepan, combine both soups, milk and wine and heat just to mix well. Add shrimp and crabmeat.
- In greased 9 x 13-inch baking dish, layer four noodles.
- Spread half cream cheese-pimento mixture over noodles and top with half seafood mixture. Repeat layers with remaining four noodles, cream cheese-pimento mixture, then seafood mixture.
- Sprinkle with parmesan cheese and bake uncovered at 350° for 45 minutes.
- Remove from oven, top with cheddar cheese and return to oven for 3 to 4 minutes, just until cheese melts.

Seafood Imperial

10 slices white bread, crust removed, cubed, divided
1 (16 ounce) package imitation crabmeat
2 (6 ounce) cans tiny shrimp, drained, deveined
1 cup mayonnaise
1 cup chopped celery
1 sweet red bell pepper, chopped
1 teaspoon dried parsley flakes
1 teaspoon lemon juice
½ teaspoon white pepper
5 eggs, beaten
3 ½ cups milk, divided
1 (10 ounce) can golden mushroom soup
¾ cup grated parmesan cheese

- Place half bread cubes in bottom of greased 11 x 14-inch baking dish.
- In bowl, combine crabmeat, shrimp, mayonnaise, celery, bell pepper, parsley flakes, lemon juice and white pepper. Spread seafood mixture over bread cubes. Sprinkle remaining bread cubes over seafood mixture.
- In large bowl, combine eggs and 3 cups milk and beat well. Slowly pour eggs and milk over bread cubes.
- Cover and refrigerate 4 to 5 hours or overnight.
- Bake covered at 325° for 1 hour.
- In saucepan, combine mushroom soup, ½ cup milk and parmesan cheese and heat just to mix well. Remove casserole from oven and pour soup mixture over casserole.
- Bake uncovered at 400° for 10 minutes.

Neptune Lasagna

3 tablespoons margarine
1 sweet red bell pepper, chopped
1 onion, chopped
1 (8 ounce) package cream cheese, softened
1 (12 ounce) carton small-curd cottage cheese
1 egg, beaten
2 teaspoons dried basil
½ teaspoon white pepper
2 teaspoons Creole seasoning
1 (10 ounce) can cream of shrimp soup, undiluted
1 (10 ounce) can cream of celery soup, undiluted
2 teaspoons dried basil
½ cup white wine
¾ cup milk
2 (8 ounce) packages imitation crabmeat, flaked
2 (6 ounce) packages small shrimp, rinsed, drained
9 lasagna noodles, cooked, drained
1 (3 ounce) package grated parmesan cheese
1 cup shredded white cheddar cheese

- Heat margarine in skillet and saute bell pepper and onion. Reduce heat and add cream cheese and stir until cream cheese melts.
- Remove from heat and add cottage cheese, egg, basil, white pepper and Creole seasoning and set aside.
- In bowl combine both soups, basil, white wine, milk, crabmeat and shrimp, mixing well.
- Butter 9 x 13-inch baking dish and arrange 3 noodles. Spread with one third of cottage cheese mixture and one third seafood mixture. Repeat layers twice.
- Sprinkle with parmesan cheese.
- Cover and bake at 350° for about 40 minutes.
- Uncover and sprinkle with white cheddar cheese and bake 10 minutes longer or until casserole is bubbly. Let stand for at least 15 minutes before serving.

Seafood

Seafood Royale

1 cup uncooked rice
2 (10 ounce) cans cream of shrimp soup
1 cup milk
⅔ cup mayonnaise
½ teaspoon salt
½ teaspoon white pepper
1 teaspoon creole seasoning
3 pounds cooked, peeled shrimp
1 (6 ounce) can crabmeat, drained
1 onion, chopped
2 cups chopped celery
4 tablespoons snipped parsley
1 (8 ounce) can sliced water chestnuts, drained
½ cup slivered almonds

- Cook rice according to package directions until fluffy.
- In large bowl, combine soup, milk and mayonnaise and mix well.
- Add seasoning, shrimp, crabmeat, onion, celery, parsley and water chestnuts.
- Fold in rice and mix well.
- Spoon into buttered 3-quart baking dish and sprinkle almonds over top of casserole.
- Bake covered at 325° for 25 minutes, uncover and bake another 10 minutes.

Lasagna Down-Mexico-Way

1 pound uncooked medium shrimp, peeled, deveined
2 teaspoons minced garlic
1 sweet red bell pepper, chopped
2 tablespoons olive oil
5 tablespoons margarine
⅓ cup flour
1 teaspoon Old Bay seasoning
1 cup chicken broth
1 (8 ounce) carton whipping cream
1 (16 ounce) jar hot chunky salsa
12 (6 inch) corn tortillas, cut in strips
1 (16 ounce) package imitation crabmeat, flaked
1 (12 ounce) package monterey jack cheese

- In skillet, cook shrimp, garlic and bell pepper in oil until shrimp turns pink. Remove from skillet and set aside.
- In same skillet, melt margarine and stir in flour and seasoning until smooth,
- On medium high heat gradually add broth and stir until sauce thickens. Stir in cream and salsa and heat thoroughly.
- Spread ½ cup of sauce in buttered 9 x 13-inch baking pan.
- Layer with half tortilla strips, half shrimp-bell pepper mixture, half crab, half sauce and half cheese. Repeat layers, leaving off last half of cheese.
- Bake covered at 350° for 35 minutes. Uncover and sprinkle remaining cheese over top of casserole.
- Return to oven for 5 minutes before serving.

Seafood

Shrimp and Artichokes

1 onion, chopped
1 cup diagonally chopped celery
1 teaspoon minced garlic
2 sweet red bell peppers, julienned
1 green bell pepper, julienned
½ cup (1 stick) butter
3 pounds shrimp, boiled, peeled, deveined
3 ½ cups cooked white rice
½ cup tomato sauce
1 (8 ounce) carton whipping cream
¼ teaspoon cayenne pepper
1 teaspoon Creole seasoning
2 (14 ounce) cans artichoke hearts, drained, halved
1 (8 ounce) package shredded cheddar cheese

- In large skillet, saute onion, celery, garlic, all peppers in butter but be careful not to brown.
- Add cooked shrimp, rice, tomato sauce, cream, cayenne pepper and Creole seasoning and mix well. Fold in artichoke hearts.
- Spoon into buttered 11 x 14-inch baking dish. Cover and bake at 350° for 20 minutes.
- Uncover and sprinkle cheese over top of casserole and return to oven for about 10 minutes.

Savory Shrimp Fetuccine

2 tablespoons margarine

⅓ cup chopped onion

1 teaspoon Old Bay seasoning

½ pound small shrimp, peeled, deveined

1 (10 ounce) can cream of shrimp soup, undiluted

½ cup half-and-half cream

½ cup mayonnaise

2 teaspoons white wine worcestershire sauce

½ teaspoon prepared horseradish

1 cup grated white cheddar cheese, divided

2 cups cooked fettuccine

1 (16 ounce) package frozen broccoli florets, cooked

- In large saucepan, melt margarine and saute onion. Add seasoning and shrimp and cook, while stirring, until shrimp turn pink, about 2 minutes.
- Add shrimp soup, cream, mayonnaise, worcestershire, horseradish and half the cheese. Heat just until the cheese melts.
- Fold in fettuccine.
- When broccoli has cooled from cooking, cut some stems away and discard. Fold broccoli into sauce. Spoon into a buttered 3-quart baking dish. Cover and bake at 350° for 30 minutes.
- Remove from oven and sprinkle remaining cheese on top. Bake 5 minutes longer.

The Captain's
Shrimp and Eggs

¼ cup (½ stick) butter
1 bunch fresh green onions and tops, sliced
5 tablespoons flour
½ cup dry white wine
1 (8 ounce) carton whipping cream
¾ cup milk
2 teaspoons dried dill weed
⅔ cup shredded cheddar cheese
16 hard-boiled eggs
1 ½ pounds shrimp, boiled, peeled, deveined
1 ½ cups fresh breadcrumbs
5 tablespoons butter, melted
¾ cup grated parmesan cheese

- In medium skillet, saute green onions in butter. Stir in flour and cook 1 minute, stirring constantly, but do not brown.
- Add wine, cream, milk and dill weed and cook on medium heat, stirring constantly until sauce thickens.
- Stir in cheddar cheese and set aside.
- Cut eggs in half lengthwise. Place eggs, yolk side up in 9 x 13-inch baking dish. Cover with the shrimp.
- Slowly pour sauce on top of shrimp.
- In bowl, mix breadcrumbs, melted butter and parmesan cheese. Sprinkle on top of casserole.
- Bake uncovered at 375° for 20 minutes or until hot and bubbly.

No Ordinary Shrimp

½ cup chopped onion

1 sweet red bell pepper, julienned

3 tablespoons margarine

2 tablespoons flour

½ teaspoon seasoned salt

¼ teaspoon white pepper

¾ cup half-and-half cream

1 teaspoon white wine worcestershire

1 (4 ounce) can sliced mushrooms, drained, optional

3 cups cooked, peeled, deveined shrimp

2 cups cooked white rice

¾ cup shredded cheddar cheese

¾ cup butter cracker crumbs

2 tablespoons margarine, melted

- In skillet, saute onion and bell pepper in 3 tablespoons margarine, but do not brown.
- Blend in flour, salt and white pepper and heat, mixing well.
- On medium heat, gradually stir in cream and worcestershire and stir until it thickens. Fold in mushrooms and shrimp.
- Place cooked rice in buttered 7 x 11-inch baking dish and spread out. Pour shrimp mixture over rice.
- Sprinkle cheese over top and combine cracker crumbs and melted margarine. Sprinkle over casserole.
- Bake uncovered at 350° for about 20 to 25 minutes or until crumbs are slightly brown.

Seafood

Tuna-In-the-Straw

1 (8 ounce) package egg noodles
2 (10 ounce) cans cream of chicken soup
1 (8 ounce) carton sour cream
1 teaspoon Creole seasoning
½ cup milk
2 (6 ounce) cans white meat tuna, drained, flaked
1 cup shredded processed cheese
1 (10 ounce) box frozen green peas, thawed
1 (2 ounce) jar diced pimento
1 (1.5 ounce) can shoestring potatoes

- Cook noodles according to package directions and drain.
- In large bowl, combine soup, sour cream, Creole seasoning and milk and mix well.
- Add noodles, tuna, cheese, peas and pimento.
- Pour into greased 9 x 13-inch baking dish. Sprinkle top with shoestring potatoes.
- Bake uncovered at 350° for about 35 minutes or until shoestring potatoes are lightly browned.

No-Noodle Tuna

1(8 ounce) tube refrigerated crescent rolls
1 cup shredded white cheddar cheese
1 (10 ounce) box frozen chopped broccoli, thawed
4 eggs, beaten
1 (1.8 ounce) box cream of broccoli soup mix
1 (8 ounce) carton sour cream
1 cup milk
½ cup mayonnaise
2 tablespoons dried onion flakes
½ teaspoon dill weed
2 (6 ounce) cans white meat tuna, drained, flaked
1 (2 ounce) jar diced pimentos

- Unroll crescent roll dough into one long rectangle and place in ungreased 9 x 13-inch baking dish. Seal seams and press onto bottom and ½ inch up the sides.
- Sprinkle with cheese and chopped broccoli.
- In bowl, combine eggs, broccoli soup mix, sour cream, milk, mayonnaise, onion flakes and dill weed and mix well.
- Stir in tuna and pimentos. Pour over broccoli-cheese in baking dish.
- Bake covered at 350° for 40 minutes or until a knife inserted near the center comes out clean. Cut in squares to serve.

Georgia-Oyster Casserole

2 quarts oysters
½ cup (1 stick) butter, divided
3 whole scallions, chopped
1 cup chopped green bell peppers
1½ cups fresh sliced mushrooms
¼ cup flour
1 (8 ounce) carton whipping cream
1 (3 ounce) package grated parmesan cheese
Freshly grated nutmeg
½ teaspoon paprika
½ teaspoon salt
Freshly ground black pepper
¾ cup seasoned breadcrumbs

- Drain oysters and set aside. In large skillet melt 2 tablespoons butter.
- Add scallions and bell pepper and saute until vegetables are tender.
- Add mushrooms and oysters and saute for 5 minutes.
- In saucepan melt 2 tablespoons butter over medium low heat. Add flour, stirring well. Slowly add cream, stirring constantly until suace thickens.
- Fold in cheese, mix well and pour cheese sauce into oyster mixture. Season with nutmeg, paprika, salt and pepper. Let simmer for 3 to 5 minutes.
- Spoon mixture into buttered 9 x 13-inch baking dish. Sprinkle breadcrumbs over top and dot with remaining butter. Place under broiler and brown until casserole is bubbling. Watch closely.

Fettuccine A La Crawfish

1 (12 ounce) package fettuccine
3 bell peppers, chopped
3 onions, chopped
6 ribs celery, chopped
1 ½ cups (3 sticks) butter
1 (14 ounce) package frozen crawfish tails, thawed, drained
2 tablespoons snipped parsley
4-5 cloves garlic, minced
1 pint half-and-half cream
½ cup flour
1 (1 pound) package jalapeno cheese, cubed

- Cook noodles according to directions. Drain and set aside.
- Saute bell pepper, onion and celery in butter.
- Add crawfish tails, simmer for 8 to 10 minutes and stir occasionally.
- Add parsley, garlic and half-and-half and mix well. Gradually stir in flour and mix well. Simmer for 30 minutes and stir occasionally.
- Add cheese and continue to stir until melted and blended. Mix fettuccine with sauce.
- Pour all into sprayed 6-quart baking dish. Bake at 300 for 15 to 20 minutes or until heated throughout.

Salads
For
Casseroles

Crunchy Chinese Slaw

1 cup slivered almonds
2 (16 ounce) packages shredded slaw mix
1 bunch green onions, sliced
1 green bell pepper, finely diced
1 sweet red bell pepper, finely diced
1 cup sliced celery
1 (11 ounce) can mandarin oranges, drained
2 packages chicken-flavored Ramen noodles, crumbled, uncooked
1 cup sunflower seeds

Dressing:
1 cup oil
¾ cup white vinegar
¾ cup sugar
2 teaspoons salt
1 teaspoon pepper
¾ teaspoon seasoned salt
2 dashes Tabasco
Ramen noodles seasoning packet

- Toast slivered almonds at 275° for about 12 minutes.
- In large bowl, combine slaw mix, toasted almonds, onions, bell peppers, celery, oranges, Ramen noodles and sunflower seeds and mix well.
- In pint jar, combine oil, vinegar, sugar, salt, pepper, seasoned salt, Tabasco and seasoning packet and mix well.
- Spoon over slaw ingredients and toss well. Refrigerate.

*This slaw can certainly be made ahead of time
and it will keep in the refrigerator for several days.*

*This recipe is so good and it will go with just about any main dish.
And it will serve a bunch of people, probably 18 to 20. The beauty
of this recipe is that you will hope you have some left-over!*

Cauliflower and Broccoli Salad

1 (8 ounce) carton sour cream
1 cup mayonnaise
1 package original Ranch dressing mix
1 head cauliflower, cut into bite-size pieces
1 bunch fresh broccoli, broken into bite-size pieces
1 (10 ounce) box frozen green peas, thawed
3 ribs celery, sliced
1 bunch green onions and tops, chopped
1 (8 ounce) can sliced water chestnuts, drained
⅓ cup sweet relish, drained
8-10 ounces mozzarella cheese, cubed
½ cup slivered almonds, toasted

- Mix together sour cream, mayonnaise and dressing mix and set aside.
- Wash and drain cauliflower and broccoli well on paper towels. They must be well drained.
- In large bowl, combine cauliflower, broccoli, green peas, celery, onions, water chestnuts and sweet relish and mix well. Add dressing and toss. Refrigerate.

This is another salad that makes a bunch, probably serving 18 to 20. It may be made a day ahead, but you would not want to keep it more than 2 or 3 days in the refrigerator. It is really a great salad for a lot of people and you have 5 different vegetables all in one bowl.

Artichoke Salad

1 envelope plain gelatin
¼ cup cold water
½ cup boiling water
1 cup mayonnaise (not salad dressing)
1 (14 ounce) can hearts of artichoke, well drained
½ (10 ounce) package frozen green peas, thawed
2 tablespoons lemon juice
1 (4 ounce) jar chopped pimentos
1 bunch green onion and tops, finely chopped
1 ½ cups shredded mozzarella cheese
½ teaspoon salt
1 teaspoon Italian herb seasoning
⅛ teaspoon cayenne pepper
½ teaspoon garlic powder
Paprika
Olives, black olives or radishes for garnish

- Soften gelatin in cold water. Add boiling water and mix well.
- Add mayonnaise and stir until smooth.
- Remove any spikes or tough leaves from artichoke hearts, chop and stir into gelatin.
- Add all remaining ingredients except paprika. Pour into ring mold and refrigerate.
- When ready to serve, slip a knife around edges to loosen from mold. Unmold onto a serving plate lined with lettuce.
- Sprinkle a little paprika over salad. You can place olives, black olives or radishes in center of ring.

Salads

Winter Salad

Dressing:

¾ cup sugar

½ cup oil

¾ cup white vinegar

1 teaspoon salt

1 teaspoon seasoned salt

1 teaspoon seasoned pepper

¾ teaspoon garlic powder

1 (15 ounce) can cut green beans, drained

1 (15 ounce) can jalapeno black-eyed peas, drained

1 (15 ounce) can shoe-peg white corn, drained

1 (15 ounce) can green peas, drained

1 (4 ounce) jar chopped pimentos

1 sweet red bell pepper, chopped

- In 3-quart container with lid, combine dressing ingredients and mix well.
- Add all drained vegetables to container and stir well. Cover and refrigerate.

All of these ingredients may be kept in the pantry, except the bell pepper and it really wouldn't hurt to leave it out. When you need a quick "something" to take to a friend, this is it! And it can be kept in the refrigerator for a week. It's a really good salad to have "on tap"!

Crunchy Pea Salad

1 (16 ounce) package frozen green peas, thawed
½ head cauliflower, cut into small florets
1 cup chopped celery
1 (8 ounce) can water chestnuts, drained
1 (4 ounce) jar pimentos, drained
1 ½ cups mayonnaise
¼ cup prepared Italian dressing
½ teaspoon salt
½ teaspoon seasoned salt
Scant ⅛ teaspoon cayenne pepper
1 cup peanuts
½ cup bacon bits

- In large bowl, combine all ingredients except peanuts and bacon bits and toss well. Cover and refrigerate.
- When ready to serve, add peanuts and toss.
- Place in a pretty crystal bowl and sprinkle bacon bits over top as garnish.

Black-Eyed Pea Salad

2 (15 ounce) cans jalapeno black-eyed peas, drained
1 ripe avocado, peeled, chopped
1 purple onion, chopped
1 cup chopped celery
1 sweet red bell pepper, chopped
1 green bell pepper, chopped

Dressing:
⅓ cup oil
⅓ cup white vinegar
3 tablespoons sugar
¼ teaspoon garlic powder
½ teaspoon salt

- In large bowl, mix all salad ingredients together. (It would be a good idea if you sprinkled a little lemon juice over the avocado as you peel it.)
- Combine dressing ingredients and mix well.
- Add dressing to vegetables and toss. Cover and refrigerate. Onion, celery and peppers will stay crisp in the refrigerator several days, so omit avocado if you don't plan to serve the same day.

Salads

Calico Salad

1 (15 ounce) can whole kernel white corn, drained
1 (15 ounce) can green peas, drained
1 (8 ounce) can whole green beans, drained
1 (15 ounce) can garbanzo beans, drained
1 cup chopped celery
1 sweet red bell pepper, chopped
1 bunch fresh green onion and tops, sliced
1 (2 ounce) jar chopped pimento, drained

Dressing:
½ cup sugar
½ cup wine vinegar
½ cup oil
1 teaspoon salt
½ teaspoon pepper
½ teaspoon basil
1 tablespoon white wine worcestershire sauce

- Drain all vegetables and combine in bowl with lid.
- Mix dressing ingredients thoroughly and pour over vegetables.
- Cover and refrigerate overnight. This will keep several days in refrigerator.

Layered Company Salad

1 package fresh spinach, torn into pieces, divided
1 cup sliced fresh mushrooms
1 bunch green onions and tops, chopped
1 (10 ounce) box frozen green peas, thawed
3 ribs celery, sliced
1 ½ cups shredded cheddar cheese
2 teaspoons sugar, divided
Salt
Pepper
4 hard-boiled eggs, grated
1 sweet red bell pepper, chopped
1 cucumber, sliced
½ head cauliflower, chopped
1 cup shredded monterey jack cheese

Dressing:
1 ½ cups mayonnaise
1 ½ cups sour cream

- For this salad, use only half the spinach for the first layer in the bottom of a large bowl, then place a layer mushrooms, green onions, peas, celery and half the cheddar cheese.
- In bowl combine mayonnaise and sour cream for dressing and spread half over top of cheese. Sprinkle with 1 teaspoon sugar, a little salt and lots of pepper.
- Next layer remaining spinach, eggs, bell pepper, cucumber, cauliflower and remaining cheddar cheese. Spread remaining dressing on top.
- Sprinkle 1 teaspoon sugar, a little salt and pepper. Top with monterey jack cheese.
- Cover with plastic wrap and refrigerate overnight.

A large crystal bowl about 10 inches in diameter is a must for this spectacular dish.

Salads

Crunchy Pecan Salad

1 (16 ounce) package frozen green peas, thawed
½ head cauliflower, cut into small florets
1 cup chopped celery
1 (8 ounce) can water chestnuts, drained
1 (4 ounce) jar pimentos, drained
1 ½ cups mayonnaise
¼ cup prepared Italian dressing
½ teaspoon salt
½ teaspoon seasoned salt
Scant ⅛ teaspoon cayenne pepper
1 cup chopped pecans
½ cup bacon bits

- In large bowl, combine all ingredients except pecans and bacon bits and toss well. Cover and refrigerate.
- When ready to serve, add pecans and toss.
- Place in a pretty crystal bowl and sprinkle bacon bits over top as garnish.

Wonderful Broccoli Salad

1 large bunch fresh broccoli, cut into small bite-size florets
½ purple onion, sliced and separated
½ cup golden raisins
½ cup slivered almonds, toasted
½ cup chopped celery
¼ cup imitation bacon bits, for garnish (optional)

Dressing:
1 cup mayonnaise
¼ cup sugar
2 tablespoons vinegar
1 teaspoon salt
½ teaspoon pepper

- Wash your broccoli ahead of time and drain on paper towels. (The broccoli needs to be well-drained.)
- In large bowl, combine broccoli, onion raisins, almonds and celery and mix well. (The sliced and separated onion looks better, but chopped onion is easier to eat.)
- Combine dressing ingredients, spoon over broccoli mixture and toss. Refrigerate several hours before serving.
- Sprinkle bacon bits over salad just before serving. (You can use the real thing if you happen to have some bacon left over from breakfast.)

When I first saw this salad I thought, "Raisins in my salad – no way!" But I was wrong. Now this is my favorite salad. Another benefit is that you can make it a day ahead. Remarkably the broccoli stays crisp for several days (however I wouldn't keep it longer than 2 or 3 days because of the mayonnaise).

Salads

Notes

Salads

Master Grocery List

FRESH PRODUCE
- ___ Apples
- ___ Avocados
- ___ Bananas
- ___ Beans
- ___ Bell Peppers
- ___ Broccoli
- ___ Cabbage
- ___ Carrots
- ___ Cauliflower
- ___ Celery
- ___ Corn
- ___ Cucumbers
- ___ Garlic
- ___ Grapefruit
- ___ Grapes
- ___ Lemons
- ___ Lettuce
- ___ Lime
- ___ Melons
- ___ Mushrooms
- ___ Onions
- ___ Oranges
- ___ Peaches
- ___ Pears
- ___ Peppers
- ___ Potatoes
- ___ Strawberries
- ___ Spinach
- ___ Squash
- ___ Tomatoes
- ___ Zucchini
- ___ _____
- ___ _____

DELI
- ___ Cheese
- ___ Chicken
- ___ Main Dish
- ___ Prepared Salad
- ___ Sandwich Meat
- ___ Side Dishes
- ___ _____
- ___ _____

FRESH BAKERY
- ___ Bagels
- ___ Bread
- ___ Cake
- ___ Cookies
- ___ Croissants
- ___ Donuts
- ___ French Bread
- ___ Muffins
- ___ Pastries
- ___ Pies
- ___ Rolls

DAIRY
- ___ Biscuits
- ___ Butter
- ___ Cheese
- ___ Cottage Cheese
- ___ Cream Cheese
- ___ Cream
- ___ Creamer
- ___ Eggs
- ___ Juice
- ___ Margarine
- ___ Milk
- ___ Pudding
- ___ Sour Cream
- ___ Yogurt
- ___ _____
- ___ _____

FROZEN FOODS
- ___ Breakfast
- ___ Dinners
- ___ Ice
- ___ Ice Cream
- ___ Juice
- ___ Pastrics
- ___ Pies
- ___ Pizza
- ___ Potatoes
- ___ Vegetables
- ___ Whipped Cream
- ___ _____
- ___ _____

GROCERY

___ Beans
___ Beer/Wine
___ Bread
___ Canned
    Vegetables
___ _____
___ _____
___ Cereal
___ Chips/Snacks
___ Coffee
___ Cookies
___ Crackers
___ Flour
___ Honey
___ Jelly
___ Juice
___ Ketchup
___ Kool-Aid
___ Mayonnaise
___ Mixes
___ _____
___ _____
___ Mustard
___ Nuts/Seeds
___ Oil
___ Pasta
___ Peanut Butter
___ Pickles/Olives
___ Popcorn
___ Rice
___ Salad Dressing
___ Salt
___ Seasonings
___ _____
___ _____

___ Sauce
___ Sodas
___ Soups
___ Spices
___ _____
___ _____
___ Sugar
___ Syrup
___ Tea
___ Tortillas
___ Water
___ _____
___ _____

MEAT

___ Bacon
___ Chicken
___ Ground Beef
___ Ham
___ Hot Dogs
___ Pork
___ Roast
___ Sandwich Meat
___ Sausage
___ Steak
___ Turkey
___ _____
___ _____

GENERAL

MERCHANDISE

___ Automotive
___ Baby Items
___ _____
___ Bath Soap
___ Bath Tissue
___ Deodorant
___ Detergent
___ Dish Soap
___ Facial Tissue
___ Feminine
    Products
___ Aluminum Foil
___ Greeting Cards
___ Hardware
___ Insecticides
___ Light Bulbs
___ Lotion
___ Medicine
___ Napkins
___ Paper Plates
___ Paper Towels
___ Pet Supplies
___ Prescriptions
___ Shampoo
___ Toothpaste
___ Vitamins
___ _____
___ _____

PANTRY

Casseroles to the Rescue

Index

C

Index

Index

Index

P

Pasta

Pork

Index

T

Index

Index

BOOKS PUBLISHED BY COOKBOOK RESOURCES

Easy Cooking With 5 Ingredients
The Ultimate Cooking With 4 Ingredients
The Best of Cooking With 3 Ingredients
Easy Gourmet Cooking With 5 Ingredients
Healthy Cooking With 4 Ingredients
Easy Slow-Cooker Cooking With 4 Ingredients
Easy Dessert Cooking With 5 Ingredients
Quick Fixes With Mixes
Casseroles To The Rescue
Kitchen Keepsakes/More Kitchen Keepsakes
Mother's Recipes
Recipe Keepsakes
Cookie Dough Secrets
Gifts For The Cookie Jar
Cookbook 25 Years
Pass The Plate
Texas Longhorn Cookbook
Mealtimes and Memories
Holiday Treats
Homecoming
Cookin' With Will Rogers
Best of Lone Star Legacy Cookbook
Little Taste of Texas
Little Taste of Texas II
Southwest Sizzler
Southwest Ole
Classroom Treats
Leaving Home

www.cookbookresources.com

To Order *Casseroles to the Rescue*:

Please send_____hard copies @ $ 19.95 (U.S.) each $_____

Plus postage/handling @6.00 each $_____

Texas residents add sales tax @ $1.22 each $_____

Check or Credit Card (Canada-credit card only) Total $_____

Charge to my ❏ [MasterCard] or ❏ [VISA]

Account # _____

Expiration Date _____

Signature _____

Mail or Call:
Cookbook Resources
541 Doubletree Drive
Highland Village, Texas 75077
Toll-free: 866/229-2665
www.cookbookresources.com

Name _____

Address _____

City _____ State _____ Zip _____

Phone (day) _____ (night) _____

- -

To Order *Casseroles to the Rescue*:

Please send_____hard copies @ $ 19.95 (U.S.) each $_____

Plus postage/handling @6.00 each $_____

Texas residents add sales tax @ $1.22 each $_____

Check or Credit Card (Canada-credit card only) Total $_____

Charge to my ❏ [MasterCard] or ❏ [VISA]

Account # _____

Expiration Date _____

Signature _____

Mail or Call:
Cookbook Resources
541 Doubletree Drive
Highland Village, Texas 75077
Toll-free: 866/229-2665
www.cookbookresources.com

Name _____

Address _____

City _____ State _____ Zip _____

Phone (day) _____ (night) _____